Interpreting God's Word in Black Preaching

by Warren H. Stewart, Sr.

Judson Press ® Valley Forge

INTERPRETING GOD'S WORD IN BLACK PREACHING

Copyright © 1984

Judson Press, Valley Forge, PA 19482-0851

The Scripture quotations in this publication are from the Revised Standard Version
of the Bible copyrighted 1946, 1952 © 1971, 1973 by the Division of Christian
Education of the National Council of the Churches of Christ in the U.S.A., and
used by permission.

Library of Congress Cataloging in Publication Data

Stewart, Warren H.
  Interpreting God's word in black preaching.

  Bibliography: p.
  1. Afro-American preaching.   I. Title.
BV4221.S73 1984   251'.00240396073   83-17552
ISBN 0-8170-1021-1

Printed in the U.S.A.
            01 02 03 04 05
13 12 11 10 9 8 7 6 5

I dedicate this book to my mother,
Mrs. Jessie Elizabeth Jenkins,
who has expressed her love to me
in so many immeasurable ways.
1 Corinthians 13:8-13

Preface

This work has been conceived and executed with my encouragement from start to finish. So it is to be expected that I would be enthusiastic in my recommendation of the finished product. My attitude at the very outset of this undertaking was based on hard data; it still applies and is well worth sharing here.

Warren Stewart seems providentially prepared to engage in this task. I know academics aren't supposed to say such things, but the evidence is overwhelming. Who else on earth could combine the following credentials for doing a definitive study on the black pulpit's hermeneutic tradition?

He worked for four years as a student assistant to Sandy F. Ray in Brooklyn. This man was the unchallenged master raconteur of the black folk Bible story. At the same time, he was very possibly the most astute preacher that ever lived when it comes to synthesizing advanced biblical scholarship with seemingly casual, unostentatious, and existentially relevant art. Since Dr. Ray never got around to analyzing his skill and committing it to writing, on whom could his mantle more appropriately fall?

At the same time, Stewart was for three years a student of James Sanders at Union Theological Seminary. This very respected Bible scholar combined marvelous new work in hermeneutics with an amazingly accurate and deeply sensitive familiarity with the black preaching tradition. I'll never forget our black response to his celebrated sermon "Joseph Our Brother," delivered to American Baptists at Boston in 1968. We simply could not contain our joy.

The next year or so, I saw Dr. Sanders at an alumni meeting and proceeded to regale him with my newly gained gems on the validity of some facets of black preaching. To my absolute amazement, he had already catalogued them on the basis of visits to black store fronts and other meeting places. He had also written glowing accounts of worship in the black Brooklyn Baptist congregation where he was a member and Gardner C. Taylor was the pastor. After listening to such powerful and poetic preaching genius, he had a right to apply terms like "experiential hermeneutic" to what he heard and felt.

It is not hard to see the impressiveness of Warren Stewart's mentors and to wonder that he should have been so blessed as to experience these two, but it is time to look at the writer himself. Here is a scholar who has practiced his subject with such power as to bring about huge growth in his own parish in Phoenix. That about which he writes so well here is no mere theory; it comes forth after having been tried with marvelous results. Of course the tradition he analyzes has been tried for generations, even centuries. But he has not let his scrutiny hurt the subject while producing a major contribution to black cultural self-understanding and to biblical hermeneutics in general.

Let me offer one word of caution and challenge. Although this work goes far beyond the bare beginnings done by the late Bishop Joseph Johnson and myself, it is still only a substantial start and a creative, useful, first nomenclature. There is much more to be done, as is the case with all first treatments of the black religious tradition. This vein, as it were, holds much more to be mined and refined and shared. Warren Stewart is impressively equipped to continue the task, but others must join him in what may well be the most significant of all black contributions to Christendom at large.

Henry H. Mitchell

Contents

Acknowledgments

My deep love for preaching and my increasing desire to know more about the "how to" questions of effective proclamation planted the seed for this book a dozen years ago. My early exposure to black preaching at its best in my years as a novice preacher in Coffeyville, Kansas, nurtured that seed. During my years at Bishop College, I was exposed to many of the finest and most gifted pulpiteers of the black church in America, and the experiences, in turn, continued to prompt the question of how effective preaching is done. During my work toward the Master of Divinity and the Master of Sacred Theology degrees at the Union Theological Seminary in New York City, I concentrated my studies in the area of biblical interpretation and hermeneutics. At Union, I was greatly influenced by the creative and insightful work in this field by Professor James A. Sanders.

After entering the Doctor of Ministry program at American Baptist Seminary of the West, Berkeley, California, I continued to cultivate this interrogative seed. The Black Church Studies program, under the direction of Dr. Henry H. Mitchell, prompted my well-nurtured seed to break ground gradually in the form of this written work. Therefore, much of what is contained in the next few pages is not necessarily "new" in the field of hermeneutics in preaching. The evolving principles are based on old ideas intertwined with my inquisitive searching to pinpoint that which is intuitively involved in my familiar tradition of effectively and accurately proclaiming the Word.

Numerous pulpiteers of the black church in America could have been used to exemplify the evolving hermeneutical principles discussed here. However, in an effort to examine with consistency some of the best of black preaching and upon the advice of my faculty, I selected the published sermons of Dr. Sandy F. Ray, late pastor of the historic

Cornerstone Baptist Church of Brooklyn, New York, and widely acclaimed as one of the most "prolific, profound, and God inspired preachers of the gospel"; Dr. William A. Jones, Jr., eminent pastor of the Bethany Baptist Church, also of Brooklyn, New York, past president of the Progressive National Baptist Convention and worldwide evangelist; and Dr. Manuel L. Scott, Sr., outstanding Texas pastor, nationally active evangelist, and a former vice-president of the National Baptist Convention, U.S.A., Inc. These preachers are known throughout America for their preaching gifts.

It should be acknowledged also that the evolving hermeneutical principles outlined in this book presuppose that anyone who would use these principles is acquainted with and knowledgeable of basic exegetical and hermeneutical skills, such as the use of commentaries, biblical language resources, and different versions and translations of the Bible. In addition, this work does not attempt to provide "how to" instructions on sermon preparation and delivery. The principles contained herein are designed to aid one in enhancing the preaching event.

Many have made willing contributions to this work in one way or another. For this I am deeply grateful and appreciative. My gratitude goes especially to:

Professor James A. Sanders, who introduced me to the field of biblical hermeneutics and its value to effective preaching;

Professor Henry H. Mitchell, for his expertise in black church studies, for his constant encouragement to pursue this work, and for his direct yet compassionate criticisms of my written work, which made me a better preacher-writer;

my Professional Peers Committee, consisting of Dr. Leland D. Hine, director of the Doctor of Ministry program, Dr. Henry H. Mitchell, and Reverend Manuel L. Scott, Jr., for providing a critique of my prospectus and first draft of my professional paper as well as for giving me helpful ideas and pointers that enhanced the content of this book;

my Lay Committee consisting of Margaret Fitzhugh, Ernest Nedd, and Robert L. Williams, Sr., who shared their valuable comments on this book from a lay perspective;

the First Institutional Baptist Church of Phoenix, Arizona, its officers and members, for providing me with total support and ample time to pursue this work while serving as their pastor, and Lewis and Catherine Huff for the special provisions they made for me, their pastor, during my studies;

Susan A. Smith, who diligently typed the rough draft and final copy of this manuscript, and Janice Engram, a faithful member of my church, who served as my initial typist, local editor, and sounding board;

Warren, Jr., and Matthew, my two sons, from whom I spent much time while working on my "doctor thing";

Serena Michele, my ever-sacrificing wife, who urged me on to the completion of this book, often at her own personal inconvenience;

and my Lord, who called me into this glorious profession and life of preaching the unsearchable riches of his grace. To God be the glory!

Warren H. Stewart, Sr.

God: The Point of Departure

Hermeneutics is an essential tool for telling the story. It may be defined as the process through which the Word of God is read, examined, interpreted, understood, translated, and proclaimed. Thus, when one is engaged in the hermeneutical process, he or she must be mindful that the final interpreter will be the audience to whom the Word will be preached. When the preached Word is understood accurately by others, then and only then can the hermeneutical process be deemed effective.

This book recognizes the central place that preaching must have in the church in order for preaching to fulfill its purpose. Therefore, it is my hope that the hermeneutical principles and ideas set forth here will inform and assist positively those in the church who have the dual task of interpreting *and* preaching the Word. While the focus of this book is on preaching in the black community, the principles would also be applicable in other parts of the Christian community.

The genius of black preaching is grounded in its almost "intuitive" ability to fulfill effectively and accurately the primary purpose of hermeneutics in biblical interpretation, which is "rightly handling the word of truth" (2 Timothy 2:15). Accurate hermeneutics in preaching determines the true effectiveness of the proclamation of God's Word.

Each chapter of this book will begin with basic theological idea(s) and point(s) that directly relate to hermeneutics in preaching. These idea(s) and point(s) will be examined in light of the black experience in religion in America. Then each evolving hermeneutical principle will be identified and succinctly outlined. Once that is done, each evolving hermeneutical principle will be illustrated and validated through excerpts from the preaching of the three noted black preachers mentioned in the acknowledgments section of this book.

Where Do We Begin?

Hermeneutics in preaching is, at the outset, a theological issue. It must not be taken for granted whose Word it is that we endeavor to interpret and proclaim. As a result, the one who engages in the hermeneutical process must confront his or her task from an appropriate theological perspective. Bishop Joseph A. Johnson addressed this matter: "Hermeneutics as wrestling with the Will and Word of God is illustrated in Jacob's wrestling at the Jabbok, Genesis 32:24-32. *Hermeneutics* presupposes that man must ultimately reckon with God." [1] For this reason, we begin this journey through the hermeneutical process with God.

God: The Point of Departure

"In the beginning God . . ." and so it is in any act of preaching and biblical interpretation. God unequivocally must be the point of departure for all exercises in hermeneutics undertaken by anyone whose calling is that of preaching the Word. It was through his divine will that humankind was inspired and moved to put into writing a summary of God's activities among us as well as a portion of God's verbalized communication with us via everything from a donkey to his only begotten Son. Because God initiated the conversation between himself and us, which is recorded within the pages of the Holy Writ, we can know more about God and ourselves. We are blessed to have at our disposal a Word that is human in form yet divine in origin. And it is this Word that provides the foundation on which all preaching can be solidly built. "In the beginning was the Word, and the Word was with God, and the Word was God" (John 1:1).

Moreover, those of us who are assigned the task of preaching in the Christian community ought to be mindful that our first and foremost responsibility for engaging in accurate and effective hermeneutics is not to ourselves, our parishioners, our denominations, or our respective alma maters. The apostle Paul in 2 Timothy 2:15 clearly identifies to whom our first and foremost responsibility is: "Do your best to present yourself to God as one approved, a workman who has no need to be ashamed, rightly handling the word of truth." In other words, the point of departure is God. It is God who made us. It is God who decided to reveal himself to us through his Word. It is God who moves persons to accept his Word as it is preached. Consequently, it is God to whom we are primarily responsible. Hermeneutics in preaching begins with God.

The fact that God is the point of departure raises a theological issue that is indispensible to those of us who preach the Word. If effective and accurate hermeneutics has God as its starting point, then how one perceives and relates to God will determine if one starts in the right direction. Hermeneutics in preaching does not begin with the text but with the *Author* of the text. What one believes about God and experiences with God informs how one interprets the text. Hermeneutics in preaching, then, is initially a theological exercise. Put another way, the first question that the biblical interpreter must ask is not "What does this text mean to me?" or "What did this text mean when it was originally written?" but *"Who is God?"* For if one does not have the correct answer to the "Who is God?" question, then that individual departs on a hermeneutical journey headed in the wrong direction.

God from a Black Perspective

Over the past decade and a half, many of the most prevalent voices heard attempting to answer the "Who is God?" question have come from members of the oppressed communities of our world. In the United States of America the most persistent, declarative, theological conversation has come from the black religious community, specifically a few black theologians and preachers. Since the late sixties, black theology has become a common and controversial topic that has affected the entire theological world. It is obvious that the echoes of the likes of James H. Cone, J. Deotis Roberts, and Henry H. Mitchell have both pricked the consciences and raised the consciousness of traditional white Anglo-Saxon Protestant theologians and those who believe and practice their pronouncements.

In addition to its generalized understanding of God's utmost concern about the welfare of *all* of his children and his creation, black theology and, more recently, liberation theology have emphasized long-overlooked elements of social righteousness that any legitimate theology must include. Any theologian who desires credibility today in recognized theological circles must advocate in some way the salient issues brought to the surface by black theology and liberation theology. It is because of the consciousness-raising contributions of these two theologies that I dare to suggest that a black angle of vision currently leads to the most accurate answer to the question, "Who is God?" In the next few pages I shall identify who God is from this perspective in a fashion essential to the fresh understanding of hermeneutics, which is the aim of this work.

First, *God is all powerful.* The word "God" evokes thoughts of an ultimate superiority, omnipotent ability, and eternal presence. God is God. In him is transcendence that is unreachable and dynamism that is indefatigable. God is the Ultimate above whom there never has been, is not, and never will be another. Nothing will ever be able seriously to challenge God for his most high position. In God is found a security that is made available to all humanity, and his power has been a major fascination of that powerless band of believers called blacks.

Picture yourself desperately ill or discouraged by poor financial investments, involved in an intense and complicated domestic problem, or discriminated against because of your color and/or your culture. Need the question be asked, ''What is the significance of having faith in an all-powerful, all-concerned God?'' There is assurance and strength in believing in a God who is present either to rescue us from an enemy or to save us from ourselves. Those who find themselves in a state of difficulty, whether momentary or perpetual, have no use for an impotent Savior or a penultimate Supreme Being whether they are black, white, brown, yellow, or red.

The religions of West Africa are characterized by their multilevel hierarchy composed of various spirits and lesser gods. However, an additional characteristic of these religions is a belief in the ''High God.'' Regardless of the powers and activities of the lesser gods and spirits, they were all accountable to the ''High God,'' the all-mighty Supreme Being who created them all and keeps everything under him in check. J. Deotis Roberts, in his book *A Black Political Theology,* pointedly summarizes the importance of an all-powerful God for black theology in the following words:

> For a black political theology, God as power is important. God as power is indispensable for a believing trust in the promises of God. It is important for an oppressed people to have the assurance that God is the only absolute source of power. Such an assurance is necessary, in order for the powerless to maintain a semblance of hope. We have overcome because we have trusted in a God of power who has brought strength out of weakness. God as power is essential to black political theology also for the reason that racism is a social evil that is built into the power structures of our society. We need a God of power to oppose the institutional racism of our society, which robs a whole people of their humanity. Where there is a power of evil, there must be a greater power for good if the victims of the evil power are to be set free. God as power is, by faith, the black man's hope of liberation.[2]

Roberts is correct in outlining the importance of a God of power for the oppressed.

Going a step further, I believe that this same omnipotent One is required by *all* races, creeds, and colors. God and his power are needed by the oppressors as well as the oppressed. The oppressors need a God strong enough to liberate them from the burden caused by their own oppression of others. An almighty God is needed to liberate them from self-righteousness, feelings of divine preference, demonically influencing an economic system, and any and all of the other manifestations of the "powers and principalities" that govern their lives. In the same vein, a God of power is essential for the oppressed minorities who need One to admonish them for lamenting their condition while doing nothing to become involved in their own liberation. This God does not unleash his power upon the oppressors' sins and then withhold it to let the oppressed do as they please. This Supreme Being's omnipotence does not play favorites, regardless of which group is morally, spiritually, and socially out of line with his will.

The God who is all powerful is powerful enough to withstand our feeble and ridiculous efforts to bribe him into being our permanent bodyguard. In the same manner, this God must be allowed to free the one who must interpret God's Word from the bondage and chains of fostering an idea of God that limits the very omnipotence of the Creator of all humankind. No effective and accurate hermeneutics in preaching can take place unless the all-powerful God is present in the mind of the interpreter of God's Word.

An ancient yet contemporary pivotal point around which black theology revolves is the idea of *God as liberator*. No other point in black theology has been so central to all of its noted advocates. To be sure, the idea of God as a liberator can be traced most notably to Moses and the Hebrew children in the Exodus event. However, close scrutiny of the Bible will reveal that most of God's activities among us relate to divine efforts to free us from the bondage and slavery that sin has placed upon us in individual, communal, cultural, national, and global settings.

Abraham was liberated from his almost idolatrous love for the son of his old age during the divinely requested sacrifice of Isaac. The Hebrews were freed from the cultural intrusions of the pagan worship of Egypt by the hand of God. The nation of Israel was emancipated from its own apostasy, hypocrisy, and idolatry when the Almighty allowed Babylon and Assyria to ravage its land and take his Chosen People into exile for their own benefit.

The New Testament, in John 3:16, informs us of God at his best in the process of our liberation as God gave his only begotten Son in order to release us from an otherwise eternal captivity called death. The resurrection event is, for the Christian community, the most significant event in the history of our Judeo-Christian heritage because of its victorious conquest over sin at its worst. Of course, the eschatological promise of the final act of liberation, which will occur at the Second Coming of Christ, provides hope for those who have lived as well as for us who yet live in him. It is that one final exodus event that will come to pass on our behalf. So the concept of God as liberator cannot be identified by stubborn exegetes and theologians as merely a theme for frustrated minorities and Third World Christians. Liberation is an active part of the divine nature.

Those who have never lived under obvious oppression are most apt to miss seeing God as a liberator. Moreover, it is usually the case that non-oppressed groups view themselves as liberated from the conditions of the oppressed. They also interpret their liberation from the conditions of the oppressed as a special blessing granted by God; yet there is hardly ever a feeling that the non-oppressed should use their liberation to liberate those around them who are oppressed. At this point black theology has been most helpful in causing the broader Christian community to recognize and accept God as being actively involved in the process of holistic liberation as it relates to individuals as well as groups.

Let it not be said that the context of blacks in America has had nothing to do with this revelation. From the oppression inflicted upon blacks who were stolen from their West African homelands and sold here as less-than-human slaves up to the ultraright conservatism of the eighties, the burdensome context is provided in which God truly has spoken as a liberator.

The oppressed members of the black community in America have almost always read and understood the Scripture in the light of God speaking to them in their context. This is not to say that their context dictated to them what God was saying through his Word. On the contrary, the oppressed black community found strength in knowing that God had been actively involved in the liberation of the Hebrew children. Thus, more than likely, God would take an active part in the liberation of black people from their oppression. In other words, they believed that the all-powerful God is aware of the human needs of a downtrodden people who were quite similar to the Israelites in Egypt. Bishop Joseph A. Johnson reflected on the Scripture and blacks in America in the following words:

> The Black experience is a religious experience in which the forefathers reinterpreted the Christian faith in the light of their experiences of exclusion and suffering. They did not just read the Bible. They brought to the Bible their total experiences—pain and pleasures, defeats and victories, their hopes and despairs, their cries, agonies and the belief that a better day is coming. They identified themselves with the oppressed Israelites and had a living experience of the God of Israel as a God of freedom and liberation, intervening and acting on their behalf. The Black Spiritual, ''Go Down Moses, Way Down in Egypt . . .'' epitomizes this belief.[3]

Does this seem to imply that one must be black in order to know

God as a liberator? Certainly not. The Scripture is permeated, as mentioned above, with the theme of liberation. A theology of freedom, justice, love, peace, human dignity, and reconciliation is essential for any and every Christian. However, this liberating quality of God does imply that every person or group that professes to believe in the God of the Christian faith must recognize the need for liberation, whether on a personal, social, or communal level. This can only be done through the process of continuous self-examination and interaction with members of the oppressed as well as the oppressors. God must be approached as a liberator by us who are bound by our cultural differences, acquired prejudices, handed-down traditions, and propensity toward homogeneity. Each of us who is assigned to interpret the Word of God for ourselves and others must first be liberated by the God of liberation. Then and only then will we realize that God as a liberator demands liberation for *all*.

In the black religious community, God is not a distant, cosmic force that provides presence and power without personality. God is a living, loving, and involved Person who never ceases to express love and concern for all of God's children. Therefore, the description of God as *a warm Personality, intimate Father, and self-giving Son* provides a positive portrait of God. Of course, it was Jesus the Christ who really "pushed" the fatherhood of God more than any other human being. Black people as a whole sincerely believe that "all of God's children" includes *every* human being. It is not necessary for members of the black religious community to take an extensive course in exegesis in order to love, respect, forgive, and pray for their brothers and sisters of different colors and cultures because they know that all of the "family of man" had but one origin, our Father-God.

There are three things I want to point out under the topic of God as a warm Personality, intimate Father, and self-giving Son. First, the *providence of God* is an applied doctrine in the black religious community as it seeks to understand who God is. God as Father means that he is not only aware of our needs but also makes sure that our needs are provided. Our Father-God does not leave us alone to struggle with the obstacles of life.

For that matter, life itself is viewed in a very positive mode. Dr. Henry H. Mitchell, in his book *The Recovery of Preaching*, commented on the black positive view of life:

> In the developmental years of West African culture/religion, it was intuited that "God is OK," and "Life is OK." No amount of absurdity and injustice seemed capable thereafter of discouraging this profound affirmation of the goodness of life.[4]

Life is good because the Creator of life is good. In spite of the inequities that life places on most blacks in so many ways, a strong doctrine of the providence of God gives hope amidst any despairing situation. The Old Testament has been the primary source for this doctrine of the providence of God. However, it must never be forgotten by the black religious community that even before their foreparents had a working knowledge of the Bible, the religion and culture of West Africa advocated a provident Father-God and the goodness of life.

Second, it is important to members of the black religious community that an attribute of God is God's *concern about wholeness.* Western religion and theology have had a tendency to compartmentalize life. Since the time of Jesus Christ and even before, the human being has been divided into "mind, body, and soul." The adjectives—physical, psychological, social, spiritual, intellectual, professional, and personal—have been used quite extensively in describing the different compartments constituting the human entity. This, in turn, has taken the emphasis away from *wholeness,* which is one with the nature of God.

In an unpublished article, J. Deotis Roberts noted some predictions about theology in the eighties, one of which says that theology will be "pluralistic" and, "The meaning of the gospel will be particularized." [5] Nevertheless, in spite of a group's particular context and the theology that arises out of that situation, the ultimate end must be *wholeness.* This is where the black religious experience has been revelatory to other more traditional theological circles, in that it views God and life integrally and holistically.

In the article just mentioned, Roberts establishes an absolute for hermeneutics arising out of the black context. He writes:

> I will now share what I perceive to be some important characteristics of a viable black hermeneutic. First, it should have a universal vision. . . . Universal, as used here, would allow for contextualization of theology in each and every culture, whether European, African, Asian or Latin American. Universal includes all cultures, all ethnics—all peoples and all religions. [6]

Black preaching addresses the needs of the whole person because God who is the source and subject of black preaching cannot be compartmentalized. His fatherhood includes divine integrity. Because God is whole, then he seeks to do what is essential to bring about our wholeness.

Thirdly, *the person of Jesus Christ* provides for a Father-God who freely became intimate with his created humanity in order to liberate us through his self-giving love. God, through his Son, came to humanity on our level. It is important also that he came as a member of an oppressed community. During his earthly tenure, Jesus Christ associated with, assisted, and exalted the disinherited as examples of persons most apt to possess the appropriate attitude to be used by God. His presence in the flesh prompts the disadvantaged to remember that their all-powerful God has experienced what they experience. On the other hand, it challenges the advantaged to recognize that there is no inherent virtue in having more material things than the majority of the rest of the world. Most of Jesus' message bears out this point. Therefore, there is strength received and direction given in knowing that the "life, ministry, death and resurrection of Jesus has radically transformed the human situation and has made possible triumphant Christian living."[7] Those who proclaim the Word must be true to the warm, intimate, and sacrificial Person whom all of His creation are blessed with the privilege to call Father.

"Who is God?" This question can be answered by almost everyone. But it has been the black religious community that has most recently reintroduced God as *all powerful, as liberator,* and *as a warm Personality, intimate Father, and self-giving Son.* Thus, from the answer to the question "Who is God?" evolves the first hermeneutical principle.

The Evolving Hermeneutical Principle

He or she who interprets and preaches the Word must *know God to be actively involved in the continuous process of humankind's holistic liberation.* This principle, then, informs the preacher as well as the text on the ultimate end of God's purpose, which is revealed through his Word. It serves as the primary criterion for insuring not only that the interpreter departs on his or her hermeneutical journey but also that the departure is headed in the right direction. All preaching in all contexts and cultures, if it would be true to God, *must* have as its end the holistic liberation of those who hear and receive it. Otherwise, according to James H. Cone, it ". . . is at best an intellectual hobby, and at worst blasphemy."[8] This principle is as appropriate for the constituents in conservative right-wing denominations and independent bodies as it is in the black church communities located in the inner cities of our urban metropolises. God must be allowed to fulfill his will that all humanity will be free to be all that they are equally made by God to be. The most compassionate act by God that manifested this hermeneutical principle was the life, ministry, death, and resurrection of God's only Son, Jesus Christ, who lived among the least of us on an intimate basis.

In the following lines, excerpts from messages delivered by the late Dr. Sandy F. Ray and Dr. William A. Jones, Jr., and Dr. Manuel L. Scott, Sr., will be examined in an effort to substantiate *Hermeneutical Principle Number One.* All of these preachers are highly respected in both black and white religious communities in America. In fact, most of the sermonic material of Ray and Scott examined for this project was published and distributed by a predominantly white Southern denominational publishing house.

Dr. Sandy Ray, in a sermon entitled "Take a Little Honey," sets the stage for a clear example of the all-powerful God by recalling the meeting of Elijah and the priests of Baal on Mt. Carmel. Israel had gone through an extended famine and drought, and a God powerful enough to overrule the weather was needed to remedy the situation. (The priests of Baal did not know that God had permitted the crisis in the first place.) Here is how Sandy Ray puts it:

> Finally, the issue was brought to focus. Elijah said the issue was not rain; it was religion. . . .
> On Mt. Carmel, the priests of Baal began their ceremonies of dancing, chanting, and prayers to Baal. . . . They had equipment and facilities, but there was no fire. Equipment and facilities in the church are terribly disappointing when there is no fire. Many churches are specializing in facilities, but short on the point of fire . . . the appearance of fire, representing the presence of God at Carmel, should arm us for those frustrating, lonely periods of opposition.[9]

Manuel Scott, Sr., illustrates God as being all powerful by relating an encounter he had with a colleague around the "Who is God?" question. Scott wrote:

> A ministerial classmate of mine is so opposed to this false conceptualization of God that he deploys cheap verbiage to voice his protest. Almost invariably when encountering him he confronts me with, "God ain't no nigger." He could well add with identical accuracy, but finer semantics, "Neither is God a white man." God is colorless, creedless, and cosmopolitan.[10]

Scott goes on to write in the next few lines:

> The Christian idea of God is not pantheistic, but panentheistic. (God is not equal to everything, but God is in everything, and yet beyond everything.)[11]

William A. Jones, Jr., in his book *God in the Ghetto*, pinpoints the Christian God based on Judaic roots.

> The revelation of God which came to the people of Israel had as its primal purpose the rule of God in human affairs.
> The public ethic of Jesus of Nazareth validated the prophetic message of the Old Covenant. The purpose of the Incarnation was to demonstrate in history that God loves the world and that religion should serve the physical and spiritual needs of people. The nature of the Messianic mission was made unequivocally clear when Jesus stood in the synagogue in Nazareth and read from Isaiah. . . .[12]

Jones brings out this liberating aspect of God in Christ in another sermon, entitled "Back-door Divinity." He preached, "Lastly, He came by way of the back door because that's the location of most of His children."[13]

Dr. Scott emphasized that the cross is a symbol of liberation in a message called "Cross Power," based on 1 Corinthians 1:18. He proclaims:

> The gospel makes the glad sounding that
>   in the cross of Christ
>   a source of power is available
> without which all other fountains of force and energy can become liabilities.
> This message sends out a call to those whose
>   capacities and abilities
>   are restricted
>   by reason of residence
>   and wicked rulers
>   to plug into the cross
> and know it to be as the text tells us, "the power of God." [14]

The fatherhood of God is made manifest in a sermonic discourse delivered by Manuel Scott, Sr., on the "Biblical Basis for Brotherhood." In speaking of the primary message of the Bible, Scott declares:

> It affirms that sisterly and brotherly affection should be maintained because we are the creatures of one Creator. "Have we not all one Father? Has not one God created us all?" [15]

The intimacy of Jesus and the providence of God both arise out of the following preached word by Sandy F. Ray:

> Jesus stands at the shore wherever humanity (hopeless, disappointed, and frustrated) may be washing their nets, saying, "Go back and try again." . . . Thanks be to God for a loving Savior who sits by the shore of every soul who is found washing empty nets. He is saying, "Go back and try again." [16]

In almost the same manner as Ray, Jones exalts the providence of God and intimacy of God in Christ:

> Jesus came to declare the presence of God everywhere. No situation was deemed off limits to the sacred presence. . . . He brought God to dusty roads and back streets, and He voiced God's concern about all human conditions detrimental to the abundant life. Wherever He went, from Capernaum to Calvary, He was engaged in fellowship with the forgotten and showed love for the least.[17]

On the goodness of creation, Jones preached, "Regardless of a man's interpretation of Genesis, he must of necessity conclude that creation is a good thing spoiled." [18] In another sermon the intimate concern of

God is expressed about the conditions of our contemporary world. Observe Jones' timely words about God:

> He's interested in slums and suburbs, preachers and politicians, the needy and the greedy. God's concerned about alleys and avenues, jet planes and jails, sinners and saints. God is upset over nuclear nonsense, political corruption, starvation, malnutrition, economic exploitation, and racial injustice. God is disturbed over the victimized masses, controlled and manipulated by a few elitists.[19]

In whatever context any interpreter of the Holy Writ finds it his or her task to preach the Word, it should never be forgotten that the need for liberation in some form is present. The outward conditions of those to whom God's message of liberation ought to be delivered may be deceptive. Therefore, hermeneutics in preaching that proves to be effective and accurate not only seeks correctly to answer the "Who is God?" question but also seeks the guidance of the Holy Spirit who can liberate the preacher from any obstacles that would keep him or her from clearly seeing the context in which he or she must speak. When this is done, the liberating process of God as made known through his Word can begin.

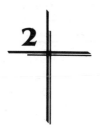

Identifying with the Word

At any given moment in our modern world, millions of persons of different colors, cultures, countries, and continents are vitally *identifying* with the Word of God as contained in the Bible. It is also very probable that many of the diverse persons and groups that recognize the Holy Writ as their guide do not recognize or identify with one another. Thus, hermeneutics in preaching God's Word must, first of all, capitalize on the extraordinary ability of the Scripture to cause peoples of practically every color and culture to identify with its content and message.

On the other hand, hermeneutics in preaching has an additional responsibility to liberate the interpreter and his or her hearers from any identification with the Scripture that establishes barriers which inhibit different and often diverse groups from identifying with one another. Therefore, in the next few pages an attempt will be made to outline a hermeneutical principle that will enable the interpreter to identify with the Scripture in such a way that his or her identification with the Word does not establish barriers and may, indeed, help to destroy barriers already built.

The Matter of Preconception

As more and more research is being done in the field of prenatal development, doctors are finding out that infants are not born into this world with "a clean slate." Their nine months in the womb allows them to develop eating and sleeping habits, and it is a fact that the mother's health—both mental and physical—has a bearing on the initial, overall health condition of the newborn infant. In one sense, an infant is born into the world "preconditioned."

So it is when the interpreter of God's Word sits down to read a text and then proceeds to discover the meaning of that text for himself or herself and those to whom its message will be directed. The interpreter does not come to the text with "a clean slate." Years of preconditioning by one's culture, color, training, and religious background are introduced to the text to be interpreted. One's psychological makeup, as well as one's sex, carries with it a certain preconditioning. Quite important are the context of the interpreter and the context of those to whom he or she will be preaching. All of which adds up to what is called preconception.

The matter of preconception should be handled with a conscious degree of acceptance. Preconception is not inherently positive or negative. However, that which one brings to an encounter with the Word of God can be an advantageous factor, depending on what has been "socially derived and socially maintained" as one's "set of preconceptions that he [or she] brings to any encounter with new suggestions or new meanings."[1] Therefore, necessary sensitivity to the fact that one does not come to the Scripture as "an empty pitcher before a full fountain" is a prerequisite for accurate and effective hermeneutics in preaching. Moreover, this sensitivity to one's own preconceptions must be a deliberate effort on the part of the interpreter. At no point should one become lax in examining and reexamining one's own preconceptions when encountering the Scripture.

The matter of preconception is connected to the previously discussed "Who is God?" question. The correct answer to the "Who is God?" question helps to liberate the interpreter from an obscuring preconception. An obscuring preconception can be a theology that emphasizes solely the grace, mercy, and compassion of God or a dogma that focuses primarily on the judgment, punishment, and eternal consequences of original sin. It can be a limited milieu that perceives God as solely concerned about the civil rights of a given cultural group. On the other hand, one's preconception can be so millenarian and eschatological that, to use a phrase frequently spoken in the black religious community, "it is so other-wordly that it is no earthly good." But God as a liberator actively involved in the continuous process of humankind's holistic liberation provides a "sensitizer" to probe one's preconception, as he or she encounters the Scripture. Once one's preconception has been reckoned with in light of *Hermeneutical Principle Number One*, then he or she is properly prepared to proceed with the hermeneutical task at hand; the next step being identifying with the Word.

The Interpreter's Context

Preconception is not the sum total of one's context. In most situations there is a direct correlation between the two. However, the mobility of people, the new emphasis on pluralism, and the massive and almost instantaneous communication systems of our supersonic age make it possible for one's preconception to be virtually unconnected to the context in which one finds himself or herself for any given period of time. For the purposes of this project it will be necessary for our usage of the word "context" to mean the "usual environment and attendant conditions and circumstances of the interpreter and those to whom his or her message is directed." This, then, implies that the bulk of hermeneutics in preaching is done by preachers who proclaim to listeners who are members of the same cultural milieu. And, I think, it is safe to say that this is a realistic assessment of most of the preaching being done in America. This assessment, of course, is not an evaluative one.

In the following lines, the context of black people living in America and their identification with the Scripture will serve as a case study of a particular cultural group that has used the Bible to enhance its otherwise despairing experience. Needless to say, it is this black experience in religion with which I am most familiar.

The African slaves who were transported to America in the eighteenth and nineteenth centuries did not land on the shores of America with "a clean slate," as far as their culture and religion were concerned. May God forgive both black and white historians who erroneously recorded that the African slaves were inhuman savages void of any legitimate religion. Indeed, it has been discovered that the ancestors of black Americans came from structured cultural backgrounds and often sophisticated religious systems. They were accustomed to communal environments. Most of them believed in and worshiped a "High God" and lesser spirits. As mentioned in chapter 1, the religious heritage of the African slaves in America informed them of a just God and the goodness of the creation. No one had to teach the Bible to them to make them aware that their oppression and inhumane treatment by their white taskmasters (and mistresses) was ungodly, unjust, and undeserved. The Africans could not accept or understand slavery as "punishment," when their only crimes were being black and getting caught by the white slave traders. The manner in which they were torn from their natural habitat, family, and community almost destroyed their sense of personhood. Nevertheless, they had an internal fortitude that outward conditions, no matter how severe, were unable to destroy. The oppressed slaves clung tenaciously to their essential cultural underpinnings and religious upbringing.

All the while these blacks were being harshly and rudely introduced to "man's inhumanity to man" at its worst, a few "Christian" slaveowners and abolitionists were beginning to introduce the Bible to the forced inhabitants of this land. In many instances, black people were instructed that God was not only aware of their enslaved condition but also approved of it. Meekness and obedience were emphasized as essential qualities of Christlikeness in "converted" slaves. If ever preconceptions established and maintained a barrier between two diverse groups who were hearers of the Word, this was it. The slavemaster's Christian religion and God, as he perceived and identified with him, were a mockery of the liberating God of the Hebrew children. The God of liberation gave hope to the slaves, while the God of the land shackled them with oppression and racism, which are still producing negative effects one hundred and twenty years after the Emancipation Proclamation. It was in this wretched context that black people identified with the Word and still identify with the Word.

For the black experience in religion, the text speaks within and to the context of those to whom its message is primarily directed. The Word of God addresses the needs of the oppressed people who seek solutions from the God of liberation for the problems and circumstances that dehumanize their very existence. However, it must be pointed out that the needs of the black people do not dictate to the text what it ought to mean. The current context is never the message. It serves as a conduit through which the message of the text comes forth. Dr. J. Deotis Roberts, in his book *A Black Political Theology,* puts it this way, ". . . this cultural milieu is the medium and not the message— it is form and not content."[2] To further clarify this point, it was hardly the case that the members of the black community during its slavery *initially* read God's Word in order to find passages that would substantiate their quest for liberation. Since a lesser form of slavery had been common in Africa, it is more than likely that they found the Scripture speaking plainly about God's desire that all persons would be totally liberated. It was this revelation, a direct result of their reading the Bible that their white masters had allowed them to read, that, in turn, enlightened them of the fact that God was not pleased with their enslavement. Thus, the text spoke within and to their life situation and not vice versa. In fact, the "revelation-in-context" of the enslaved black people was obscured from the perception of most of the whites who professed to be Christian during the antebellum period. Again, Roberts comments on this very issue in the following words:

> When African slaves were introduced to the Bible, they were able to derive meanings from it that were hidden to their oppressors. They understood God against the background of traditional beliefs in a Supreme God. They were aware of the power and moral integrity of God. Jehovah, as described in the Old Testament, was a close facsimile of the African

Supreme Being they had known. . . . As the black oppressed facing daily the white oppressors, the Exodus took on a political as well as a religious meaning.[3]

The Scripture met the needs of a people within their context. Moreover, it is often one's context that makes one ready to receive God's message without preconceptions imposed by others.

A necessary question is raised as a result of the findings mentioned in the preceding paragraph, "How did the enslaved black preacher interpret the Word accurately without the use and knowledge of exegetical skills and biblical scholarship?" Dr. Henry H. Mitchell, in his book *The Recovery of Preaching,* answers this question in the following words: "I want to suggest that the Black preaching tradition has for generations, even centuries, reached these depths intuitively, almost always without the preacher being aware of how or why."[4] In other words, there is hardly a *logical* explanation as to how the black preacher engaged in accurate hermeneutics. Nevertheless, a combination of belief in the authority of the Word that he or she preached and of the experiences through which bondage had caused the oppressed preacher to live created the climate for effective and accurate hermeneutics in preaching. Thus, the preached Word was extracted from the Bible and exalted the God of liberation who was actively involved in the liberation of the black people in an unjust society (supposedly founded upon "liberty and justice for all"). In addition to this "intuitive hermeneutic," or perhaps, intertwined with it, the unction of the Holy Spirit must be given credit as being actively involved in the liberation of the preacher from contextual influences and preconception that could easily obscure the message of the Word of God from the people to whom the preaching is directed.

Effective preaching must meet the existential needs of those to whom it is directed. Keep in mind, however, that the existential needs of any group regardless of race, color, or culture are addressed by the gospel in a way that leads to the group's holistic liberation. And at this point, Western theology and preaching have taken a back seat to the black preaching tradition. Bishop Johnson expounded, "As simple and as obvious as this may sound, the fact is that most preaching in *all* cultures today ignores people's deepest human needs."[5] Preaching cannot limit itself to one's *spiritual* needs, for there are no spiritual needs in this life that are not incarnated within the holistic needs of humankind. The human being is a complex and comprehensive living entity that was made by God. In the beginning God made a human being, not a mind, body, and soul. Consequently, preaching must address itself to the holistic needs of the human being.

With this in mind, hermeneutics in black preaching involves the following:

> The Black preacher does not merely use the Bible but rather he permits the Bible to use him. He confronts the stories of the Bible with some significant questions like: "What is this passage of Scripture saying to me about the condition of God's people?" "What answers to today's problems may be culled out of the Biblical story?" "Will this passage of Scripture bring healing to Black people who have been hurt in life and crushed by the materialistic impersonal forces of our mechanical, industrial world?" "Will this Scripture bring comfort to those who are dying and cheer to those who mourn thereby giving them the courage to "Hold on to God's Unchanging Hand" in spite of life's vicissitudes?" These are some of the questions which the Black preacher uses to interpret Scriptures. And in order to receive the answers he has mastered the art of wrestling with Scriptures.[6]

In a concluding word on this subject, the message and ministry of the late Dr. Martin Luther King, Jr., is an excellent contemporary example of preaching meeting the existential needs of those to whom it is primarily directed.

Principles of Identification

There are three principles of identification that facilitate the appropriate identification with the Word by any given cultural group. As noted previously, one group's identification with the Scripture must not build up any barriers with another group that identifies with the same Word. These three principles will provide the ground rules to prevent such divisive hermeneutics. These principles provide the basis for the evolving hermeneutical principle that shall be set forth in the next section of this chapter.

Empathetic Application

Henry Mitchell has written for several years about the "eyewitness account" that has been a trademark of most of the best black preaching. In one of his published lectures delivered on the occasion of the Lyman Beecher Lectures on Preaching at Yale Divinity School, Dr. Mitchell wrote, "Greatness in the Black pulpit almost invariably involves the ability to get into parts, especially biblical parts, with as much ease and impressiveness as one gets into one's own."[7] The preacher, as he or she becomes involved in the hermeneutical exercise, "internalizes" the story of the text, especially if the text is a biblical narrative, to the point that he or she becomes an "eyewitness" reporter, if, indeed, not one or several of the characters involved in the text. An *empathetic application* of the text and/or its characters is carried out by the inter-

preter. He or she becomes a member of the Hebrew children in Egypt
or Elijah battling the prophets of Baal or Jacob wrestling with an angel
or the demoniac roaming the Gergesene country or Pilate washing his
hands of Jesus' sentence or Paul struggling with his old nature or any
other character who arises from a passage of Scripture.

Once this saturation or identification process takes place in the mind
of the interpreter, the ancient experience can be recreated in the contemporary setting of the interpreter. Also the black preacher does not
always identify with the heroes in a passage. Quite often it is the
struggles and disappointing circumstances of a text that speak most
appropriately to the black preacher and his or her people. Moreover, it
should be noted that the preacher must be able to transmit this eyewitness
account experience to those to whom his or her message is directed in
order that they, too, can engage in *empathetic application* of the text.
The significance of this principle to effective preaching in any context
is brought out in the following statement by Mitchell:

> I have long referred to this phenomenon as the "eyewitness account."
> Anything short of such a complete rerun can hardly generate an experience
> that teaches and moves persons. "Eyewitnesses" describe settings that are
> vivid and familiar. Congregations quickly visualize and relate to the sit-
> uation, moving into the experience.[8]

The end result of the eyewitness account is to allow the listeners
almost to forget that the text was written centuries ago. They become
eyewitnesses themselves to the incident described in the text, and they
identify with the characters of the text as well as the text itself. In other
words, the experiences arising from the text become the listeners'
experiences via *empathetic application*. Bishop Johnson writes that
when this is done effectively (in reference to Jesus Christ), ". . . it is
Christ Himself walking through the congregation as God's word addressed to man."[9]

Another probable reason that the black preaching tradition has so
effectively identified with the Word through the eyewitness account
principle is that the context of the black preacher and his or her community has been, until the last forty years, primarily *rural* rather than
urban. Moreover, even in the black church commmunities of the urban
metropolises of this country, the black church has been made up of
migrated Southern blacks and persons who have vital roots in rural
black life and culture. Thus, the black preacher, to a great extent, has
not had the problem of the white preacher, as identified by Richard L.
Rohrbaugh in his book *The Biblical Interpreter:*

> . . . the biblical literature of both Old and New Testaments was written

in and to agrarian societies and preindustrial cities but is being interpreted today (at least in most American churches) in industrial societies in which the social perception of reality is markedly different from that of the biblical period.[10]

I would dare say that most black preachers do not look at Scripture from an industrial perspective because their roots keep them (and those to whom their message is directed) somewhat acquainted with the ancient agrarian culture of the biblical period. In addition, the usage of the eyewitness account and familiarity with agrarian life-style enable the interpreter and his or her listeners to become aware of the ancient context of the biblical passage being preached. This, in turn, assists the modern listeners in recognizing the original points scored by the writers of the text.[11]

Mirrors for Identity

James A. Sanders, a widely respected biblical scholar and dynamic preacher, has made significant contributions to the subject of hermeneutics in preaching during recent years. One hermeneutical principle, which he identified in an article entitled "Hermeneutics," is this: "Most biblical texts must be read, not by looking in them for models for morality, but by looking in them for mirrors for identity."[12] "Mirrors for identity" suggests that the biblical interpreter must see himself or herself in the text. This is to be done regardless of the "morality" of the characters in the text or those to whom the text was originally directed. When this is done, the interpreter and his or her audience can see themselves reflected in the Bible as a "mirror of identity." Sanders further comments:

> And this may be done by reading the story not as though it were of events way back there about ancient folk but by reading it dynamically, identifying with those who provide us the best mirrors of our identity.[13]

It should be added that the best "mirrors for identity" are not necessarily the "good guys" in any given biblical passage. It is quite often the case that biblical characters like Adam and Eve, Pharoah, Ahab, Jezebel, Nebuchadnezzar, Herod, Pilate, and the rich young ruler provide the "mirrors for identity" that most clearly reflect our real selves. This principle, therefore, implies the necessity of honesty in the interpreter as he or she examines the Word for a message from the Lord.

Utilizing the Constitutive and Prophetic Hermeneutic Modes

Professor Sanders identifies two basic hermeneutic modes, namely, (1) the constitutive and (2) the prophetic, which have been utilized in identifying with the Word.[14] In biblical times, the constitutive reading of the Torah story, which was based on a supportive interpretation of the Word, gave Israel an identity and a purpose. As the moral as well as the historical context of Israel changed, Israel became in need of a challenging message that would call it back to its original purpose as God's elect. Israel, in such a state, was not in need of a supportive reading of the tradition. The establishment context of Israel called for a prophetic interpretation of the Torah story. Israel needed to be challenged to cease its national arrogance and to pursue its divine purpose. Only a prophetic hermeneutic could recall Israel to a program of obedience. Therefore, it can be understood that the context of Israel was a determinative factor for deciding which hermeneutic mode would be used by the biblical writers. Furthermore, the misreading of the context by the interpreter usually led to the constitutive hermeneutic mode being used when a prophetic mode was necessary.

The biblical interpreter today has the responsibility of discerning correctly his or her context in order to know which hermeneutic mode is required. In his sermons, James A. Sanders uses the prophetic hermeneutic mode more often than not. This is due to Sanders' belief that the church today is analogous to Israel during the period of the classical prophets. In a lecture entitled "Jeremiah and the Future of Theological Scholarship," he said, ". . . the church today has been invaded by secularism and taken captive by the dominant culture of Western society."[15] It must also be mentioned that most of Sanders' preaching and writing are directed to middle-class, white Anglo-Saxon Protestants.

In the black preaching tradition, there is a definite need to use *both* hermeneutic modes as categorized by Sanders. As a matter of fact, in much of the best black preaching there is a *dual* usage of both the prophetic and the constitutive hermeneutic modes. If, indeed, a black preacher is speaking about the God of liberation who is on the side of the oppressed, he or she would be using the constitutive mode within the black community. That same hermeneutic mode attacks those whose life-style, system, and religion perpetuate oppression in any form or, at least, those who do not see their Christian commitment as primarily concerned about the holistic liberation of all people. The latter, then, would be addressed in the prophetic hermeneutic mode.

On the other hand, a solely constitutive hermeneutic mode would cripple the black religious community, which is guilty of wrongs committed against itself. In addition, a constitutive hermeneutic mode that would cause members of the black community to practice "reverse discrimination" toward former white oppressors is just as wrong as antebellum slaveowners justifying the slavery system by using Noah's curse of Ham and Paul's letter to Philemon. Probably the best way to make sure one interprets the Word in the appropriate hermeneutic mode is to make sure the preacher knows well the context of those to whom the message will be directed.

Sanders suggests how this can be done in the following lines:

> So one of the first hermeneutic techniques we can use to employ prophetic critique in application of a text is dynamic analogy. We should look for the persons and figures in it who might represent different folk today dynamically. Dynamic analogy means we can read a text in different ways by identifying with different people in it. [16]

Going a step further, an excellent safety valve for the interpreter would be initially to apply the prophetic hermeneutic mode to the text that he or she will be delivering in context. This may insure a dual usage of the two modes in order that the message delivered may be both supportive and challenging to those to whom it is directed. There is not one person or group alive that is following so perfectly God's desire for the holistic liberation of all people (including their own) that a *dual* usage of the prophetic and constitutive hermeneutic modes would be inappropriate.

The Evolving Hermeneutical Principle

He or she who interprets and preaches the Word must *identify with the Word in such a way that the Word will both support and challenge those to whom the message is directed.* This principle would accomplish both of the concerns for hermeneutics in preaching as spelled out in the first paragraph of this chapter. In the first place, identifying with the Scripture in a supportive mode should not alienate any person or given group from its content. Secondly, identifying with the Word both constitutively and prophetically in order to align with God's ultimate purpose of the holistic liberation of *all* humanity will not establish barriers with other persons or groups who are doing likewise and will lead to the destruction of any barriers that have been built due to divisive hermeneutics in preaching.

William A. Jones, Jr., in Part II of his book *God in the Ghetto,* exemplifies *Hermeneutical Principle Number Two* through the preaching of God's Word. In his sermon, entitled "Back-door Divinity," arising from Luke 2:7, he outlined three points that evidence the *dual* usage of the constitutive and prophetic hermeneutical modes. He expresses his first point thus:

> He came by way of the back door to avoid and to assault the arrogance of power. . . . It is conspicuous in corporate boardrooms, at command

levels in the military, in the halls of academia, in the chambers of government, and among the so-called princes of the Church. This craving for power is also present at lower levels.[17]

Jones proceeds to illustrate the second point in this sermon in the following words:

> He came that way for another reason. That was the only door that would bid Him "welcome." A soul in beggar's apparel, although a King, would elicit no warm response at the front door of sinful humanity. Herod, you remember, was a member of the front-door crowd; and as soon as he heard of His arrival, he sought to kill Him. How vivid is my own memory of the absence of front-door hospitality in this land, that shameful period when certain of us, on account of color, were considered fit only for back-door divinity.[18]

In the preceding words, one not only sees Jones' dual usage of the supportive and challenging hermeneutical modes, but one also perceives the "eyewitness account" experience when Jones relates the "back-door" struggles that he experienced by being black in America to the "back-door" entry of Jesus Christ Incarnate. From there Jones moves on to his third point, which is constitutive for most of the world and prophetic for those who have power. Jones preaches:

> Lastly, He came by way of the back door because that's the location of most of His children. . . . My main concern is to lift up the truth about God's concern for the whole of humanity, and the unalterable, undeniable reality is that most of His children are back-door dwellers.[19]

In a message based on John 1:14, Dr. Jones proclaimed:

> The Christian faith is often charged with being esoteric and ethereal, a religion so heavenly minded that it's no earthly good. Certain critics, historically and presently, have looked on Christians and accused them of espousing an ethic that is tragically divorced from the problems and pains of this world, and the charge is not without some basis in fact.[20]

This statement recognizes the need for a Word that identifies with the existential needs of those to whom it is directed. It also challenges *any* group that practices the Christian faith without becoming actively involved in the process of holistic liberation. In a cutting prophetic word, Jones declared:

> God has not declared the world off limits to Himself nor to His Church. That is our doing, not His! We have divorced faith from ethics. We have separated pulpit and pew from the public square. . . . Our witness has become bifurcated and truncated.[21]

Jones espouses the first two hermeneutical principles presented in this book in the following sermon entitled "On Prophets and Potentates." Here are his words:

> There are others among us who believe sincerely that the Gospel speaks to every human situation, that no segment of existence is off limits to spiritual scrutiny. This is a holistic view of religious faith. We make the claim that every soul should be subject unto the higher powers, but only insofar as the state's behavior coincides with the purposes of God.[22]

He prophetically as well as constitutively continues, "The Christian's first loyalty ought always be to God and not to government."[23] This supports those who are Christian and oppressed by their governments as well as challenges those who are Christian and in power to influence their governments.

In 1971, Manuel Lee Scott used Jonah as a point of departure for his book, entitled *From a Black Brother*. From "Jonah's Sermon at Nineveh," Scott alluded to the universal need for holistic liberation:

> Whatever else may be the goal of the preacher's proclamation, it aims, essentially, at changing things as they are and converting them into things as they ought to be. He speaks in the unmitigated optimism that no man needs to stay the way he is and that no condition has an immunity against change.[24]

Quite surprisingly, Scott, in this book, pronounces some sharp prophetic denouncements on members of his own black clergy. He writes, "The preaching fraternity of the Negro community is assailed by the same powerful temptations which did so easily beset the Jewish religious leadership in the time of Jesus."[25] Continuing, Dr. Scott honestly portrays the weakness of the black Baptist community:

> That the Negro church is conspicuously and catastrophically divided is too obvious for argument. Negro Baptist churchmen, especially, constitute a "broken brotherhood," a testimony to our incapacitation to bear the burden of freedom.[26]

In his second book, which is a book of sermons, Scott attempted to identify with the Word in context when he categorized his messages as *The Gospel for the Ghetto*. The sermon, "The Ultimate in Urban Renewal," is founded upon Paul's famous "new creation" formula in 2 Corinthians 5:17. Observe how Dr. Scott attacks the problem of holistic liberation.

> No sane person would argue that physical and psychological improvements are necessary and desirable. Yet, few have the courage and comprehension to affirm that the deepest need of our metropolises is not
> new houses, but a new humanity; not
> new employment, but new employers; not

new educational facilities, but new people to educate; not
new transportation, but new pedestrians; and not a
new metropolis for the man, but a new man for the metropolis.
The call for a new being and a new generation is urgent and desperate.[27]

This well-known preacher is not shy at launching an attack upon the
shortcomings in the theology and preaching of his black brothers (and
sisters). "Unbrotherly Brothers" serves as an indictment upon any
Christian person or group whose theology builds a barrier between other
persons or groups who identify with the same Word. Scott begins his
declaration thus:

> It is painful to contemplate the sins of omission and commission indulged
> in by those outside of the ghetto which make life all but unlivable by those
> in the ghetto. However, it places me under more pressure
> to ponder the ills inflicted
> by the people of the ghetto
> upon each other.[28]

Continuing his prophetic pronouncement upon the "advantaged"
members of the black community, Scott uses Moses as an example of
one who assisted his disadvantaged brethren. The example is based on
Exodus 2:13.

> The opening act in the story
> mirrors that Moses
> did not allow his personal blessings
> to blind him to the burden of his brethren.
> Affluence,
> academics,
> and aristocracy
> did not alienate his affection
> nor strangle stimulating concern
> for the less fortunate members of his race.
> In spite of his place in Pharaoh's palace and profits from the existing
> power structure, he initiated and established contact with his Hebrew
> fellows.
> He took time and effort to see their plight and know their predicament.
> He made his advantages available for their advancement. . . .
> If persons with plenty
> who have ethnic ties with overburdened groups
> were characterized by Moses' meekness and mercy
> the lot of the
> loaded down would let up.[29]

The late Sandy F. Ray was thirty years older than Jones and Scott.
Nevertheless, in a subtle and penetrating way Dr. Ray's preaching
exemplified *Hermeneutical Principle Number Two* admirably. Moreover, Sandy Ray was not gifted with a resounding voice as William

Jones or with the noted, yet genuine, pulpit gestures of Manuel Scott. However, in a fashion unique to Sandy Frederick Ray, he was able to proclaim prophetically and richly the Word of God as he saw it, identifying it with his people and helping his people to identify with it. In his sermon "Journeying Through a Jungle," Dr. Ray described the dangers that lurk in our society today.

> The modern jungle is fashionable and fabulous. It is extremely attractive with glaring lights and fascinating entertainment. The jungle is often financed by millions of dollars and protected by bribery. . . . The captains who control the jungle oppress the poor, underprivileged, underpaid, exploited, ghettorized, and untrained.[30]

Dr. Ray, in the above words, was identifying the lot of his people with "the wilderness of Judea" in which John the Baptist came preaching.

In the sermon entitled "The Testimony of a Towel," based on John 13:4, Sandy Ray exalts Jesus' pragmatic and prophetic lesson to his disciples on humility and servanthood. He preached:

> If we remove the towels from our culture, it would collapse. The titles would perish if there were no towels. The towel brigade on farms, in factories, sanitation, firemen, policemen, in kitchens, laundries, office workers, truck drivers, plumbers, electricians, and many other unheralded and non-titled keep our society moving.[31]

He continued:

> When Jesus returns, he will not be seeking titles; he will be checking towels. . . .
> Our arrogant, titles-rank-happy culture desperately needs the warm, poised, calm seasoning of true humility. This should emerge from people who claim Jesus as their Lord.[32]

Joshua 17:13-18 provides the text for one of my favorite sermons by Dr. Ray, "The Challenge of the Wood Country." Ray leads his audience in identifying with the constitutive and prophetic hermeneutical modes simultaneously:

> Joshua could well have been speaking to black people in this country at this point in time. In our frustration, much of our effort is concentrated upon struggling for "local plots" among the tribes. Some of the powers of the system have led some of us to believe that our success depends upon feeding on the weaker tribes.[33]

In an encouraging word, he further proclaimed:

> The "wood country" is not far from where we are. It is in our streets where there are crime, dope addicts, dope pushers, pimps, prostitution, hunger, sickness, racism, exploitation, slums, corruption, arrogance, and indifference. The "wood country" consists of many of our famishing

black colleges in the nation. . . . Great people were the founders of our black Baptist colleges.[34]

A closing prophetic word delivered by Dr. Ray can be found in his eloquent sermon, entitled "Take a Little Honey." Honey, for Ray, was the sweetness of humility and kindness, which help to build relationships rather than separating them. Thus, Ray preached:

> For many years, England, France, and America have ignored the Arab nations, Africa and other so-called "underdeveloped" nations. But in the grip of an energy and oil crisis we are turning to these countries which have natural resources that we desperately need.
>
> We have money, skill, diplomacy, sophistication, military power, but all of these can be bitter, sour, and cold without a little honey. Honeyless negotiations are usually short-lived. A little honey can sweeten all of our relationships.[35]

The preaching of Jones, Ray, and Scott vividly exemplifies the need for those engaged in serious hermeneutics in preaching to identify with the Word in order that it may be free to both support and challenge those to whom the message is directed. This hermeneutical principle provides a further step in moving every Christian believer toward active involvement in God's continuous process of holistic liberation for all humanity.

3

Creating an Experience with the Word

One of the salient characteristics of hermeneutics in black preaching is the preacher's art of creating the atmosphere whereby the preacher and the listener can *experience* the Word rather than merely hear it. This strong identification with the Word makes for more effective preaching because the preacher becomes the Word-incarnate. The apostle Paul alludes to this experience in 2 Corinthians 3:3: "and you show that you are a letter from Christ delivered by us, written not with ink but with the Spirit of the living God, not on tablets of stone but on tablets of human hearts." Of course, Paul makes reference to the exemplary lives of the Corinthian Christians in this passage. In actuality, he was commenting on their commendable ministry that was manifested in words and deeds. Nevertheless, during the act of preaching, the preacher ought to become the "letter" from God delivered to the people. When this is done, the messenger becomes more than a mere delivery boy or girl. On the contrary, he or she becomes part and parcel of the Word being preached. Furthermore, the desired goal is to create an experience in which the listeners can become the Word-incarnate themselves.

Because preaching involves the act of creating an experience with the Word, it can accurately be referred to as an art. The varied gifts and talents that are given to any and every preacher are to be used creatively in producing a hermeneutical and homiletical masterpiece. In his important book *The Recovery of Preaching,* Dr. Henry H. Mitchell clearly states the necessity for creating an experience with the Word: "The goal of Black preaching is to recreate a meaningful experience which communicates transconsciously, nourishing the whole human being. This is indeed high art." [1]

This chapter will outline the methodology involved in creating an experience with the Word and identify an evolving hermeneutical principle that will inform all who are commissioned to interpret and preach the Word of God.

The Process of Internalization

The first step in internalizing the Word to be preached begins with the preacher himself or herself. This step is closely related to the "eyewitness account" experience touched on in chapter 2. The preacher must become intimate with the particular scriptural passage that he or she seeks to interpret. Through *empathetic application* the preacher takes on the role(s) of the different character(s) in the passage or those to whom it was originally directed. The ancient story becomes his or her story. The situation of the text becomes the context of the preacher. The strengths and struggles, the defeats and victories that are contained in the Word are internalized in the mind of the preacher. The experiences of the past are relived in and through the preacher who is involved in effective and accurate hermeneutics in preaching. Substantiating what I have said, Dr. Mitchell writes:

> The story must be internalized in the preacher, peopled by characters he has known for years and for whom he has such deep feelings that he can authentically recreate the action and communicate the experience. A kind of saturation is required.[2]

Once internalization takes place, the ancient Word is realized as the *living* Word. The content and message of the text no longer remain as a mere historical account of a historic event in the epochal record of humankind's salvation. The Word takes on life and vitality (or better said, the interpreter becomes *aware* of the life and vitality innate in the Word of God). This is one of the primary reasons that the Bible has not been relegated to dusty bookshelves as have many other sacred writings. The Word of God contained in the Holy Writ is the *living* Word—breathing, moving, strengthening, enlightening, correcting, and saving. Therefore, whenever it is preached, it cannot be interpreted and proclaimed as the *dead* letter.

The whole process of hermeneutics in preaching revolves around making the Word *live* among the people to whom it is directed. Preaching, then, is more than an exegetically sound and expository discourse of the age-old events of persons who lived in the Holy Land centuries ago. Preaching can never be solely a lecture or speech on the profundity or simplicity of the "good life" expressed by noted personalities of countless yesterdays. Preaching, when the Word is internalized by the preacher, becomes a *living* experience, first to the preacher and then to those to whom the message is directed. Bishop Joseph Johnson informs us that black preaching values this experiential process highly. He writes:

. . . Black preaching is by its nature a story-telling process. And Black preachers have mastered the art of breathing life into both the story and the truth that it teaches. He uses his imagination creatively and he places himself as an eye witness to the story which he narrates and has mastered the art of role-playing. Therefore, it is not anything new to hear a Black preacher say, "I saw John on the Isle of Patmos, early one Sunday morning," or "I was in the Spirit on the Lord's Day," . . .[3]

As shall be pointed out when the preaching of Sandy Ray, Manuel Scott, and William Jones is examined toward the end of this chapter, the black preacher has used this process of internalization of the Word to his or her advantage and that of his or her people. It is not unusual to experience a black preacher having a first-person conversation with God about his or her calling to the ministry on Mt. Horeb in front of a burning bush or concerning his or her retreat to the desert because no one is standing up for Jehovah amidst the confrontations with the prophets of Baal or dealing with a courageous testimony before the Nebuchadnezzars of society who have warned all believers in Jehovah to be still or be killed or describing a clandestine confession before the Master somewhere on the outskirts of Jerusalem at midnight. It seems so easy for the black preacher to move from the third-person, story-telling process to first-person role playing.

For example, I remember hearing about a remark a visitor made to a young pastor after attending his church for two consecutive Sundays. The first sermon she heard the young man preach dealt with Daniel in the lion's den, and the following message dealt with Jonah fleeing from his assigned mission. In both sermons the minister internalized the main characters, Daniel and Jonah respectively. After the second sermon had been preached, the visitor remarked to the preacher, as he greeted the members and guests following the service, "Reverend, I enjoyed your two soliloquies on Daniel and Jonah. However, the next time I visit your church, I would like to hear more from *you*." I suppose it should be said here that one can overdo anything, even the internalization of the Word! On the other hand I think the sister was attempting to compliment the young man for his effectiveness at role playing, in spite of her attempt to impress him with her analysis of his soliloquies.

All of what has been stated so far in this chapter points to the fact that in order to create an experience with the Word, the preacher must become the Word-incarnate, at least to some degree. The next matter at hand is that of making the Word incarnate in those to whom the Word of God is directed.

Making the Word Incarnate in Others

It is one thing for the Word to be *alive* in the one who proclaims it; it is another thing, however, to cause that same Word to become incarnate in those to whom the message is given. Yet that is an essential part of effective and accurate hermeneutics in preaching. It is not enough for the preacher alone to be edified by the Word with which he or she becomes intimate. No matter how vivacious and exhilarating the internalization process is, the preacher's hermeneutics must proceed from him or her to those to whom the proclamation is directed. For God's message channeled through the preacher as an instrument must be delivered to the people in order that they can know and identify with the God of liberation who is actively involved in the holistic liberation of all human beings. The task is a weighty one because if the preacher cannot effectively and accurately interpret and deliver God's message to those in need of it, *then who can?* Making the Word incarnate in those who will receive the Word involves, at least, two steps once the proclaimer has internalized the Word.

The first of the two is that of *creating an emotional-intellectual experience among those who hear the Word preached.* It has long been assumed that the members of the black religious community thrive and survive solely on the emotional experiences that they receive Sunday after Sunday from "fire and brimstone" preaching and "high intensity, high volume" gospel singing.

Just recently I overheard a conversation between two well-known preacher-pastors from the West Coast. Both are considered to be intellectually astute in their preaching styles, not depending upon the traditionally black intonational climax (in other words, they don't "whoop"). The one said to the other, "Doctor, our people in our black churches today are *anti-intellectual.* They don't appreciate your and my type of message. They are just *anti-intellectual,* I tell you." The other replied, "I don't agree with that, Doctor. . . ." And I say, "Amen," to the response of the latter of the two men, both of whom are close colleagues of mine. The point is that people want a coherent, understandable experience that affects both the mind and the heart.

It is a travesty and gross injustice to imply, let alone indicate, that the slave, brought to America from Africa and introduced to the Christian faith, was ever *anti-intellectual.* Moreover, with the strides in education and technology as well as the ubiquitous presence of the television in the homes of even the poorest members of the black community, it is almost shameful to speak of an entire group of people as being *anti-intellectual.*

By common definition an "intellectual" is "one who possesses and uses intelligence.'' The word ''intellect'' may be defined simply as ''the power of understanding.'' By these definitions the black religious community as a whole has never been *anti-intellectual!* Quite the contrary, the survival tactics and intuitive hermeneutics of black people living in America under the oppression, discriminatory practices, and racism of white Anglo-Saxon Protestants have proven that black people are *highly intellectual* in the *weightier* issues of human existence, namely, survival and religion. The ability to know God as a liberator *is* in part an *intellectual* experience. Identifying with the Word *is* in part an *intellectual* experience. And it does not take a diploma or a scholastic degree to exercise the mind or to show its intelligence and understanding.

Again, returning to the first step in leading the hearers of the Word to internalize the Word, Bishop Johnson points out:

> The Black congregation wants to have an emotional-intellectual experience. They want to be helped. They want to be fed and they want to be inspired for the living of these days. Whenever this type of preaching is done before a Black congregation, creative dialogue takes place, which represents the epitome of Black worship.[4]

An emotional-intellectual experience is the initial step required to cause a congregation to internalize the Word. In other words, the hearts and minds of those persons to whom the Word is directed must be engaged in a creative experience. Their feelings as well as their understanding are to be involved in an intimate relationship with the Word of God. One without the other cannot create the climate for an authentic experience. The story that is told by the preacher must live emotionally *and* intellectually in the person(s) to whom the message is directed. Professor James H. Cone in his book *God of the Oppressed* emphasizes the importance of this emotional-intellectual experience in these words:

> In black churches, the one who preaches the Word is primarily a storyteller. And thus when the black church community invites a minister as pastor, their chief question is: ''Can the Reverend tell the story?''[5]

This story-telling criterion for the black pastorate accentuates the high level on which the proclamation of the Word is placed within the black religious community. I would dare say that if non-black religious groups in America would reelevate the preaching experience to a similar height, church-growth seminars and programs would become virtually unnecessary. Nevertheless, the creating of an emotional-intellectual experience provides a platform on which to move to the more important second step.

The second step in moving the hearers of the Word toward an experience with the Word is that of *creating a living experience among those to whom the message is directed.* Another way of putting it is: as the Word has become incarnate in the preacher, the preacher, in turn, must create the climate for the Word to become incarnate in the people. It should be noted at this point that a basic presupposition is that no effective and accurate hermeneutics in preaching can take place without the aid of the Holy Spirit. Henry Mitchell confirms this presupposition as follows:

> . . . it was late in the development of the New Testament that John (14:26) recorded a statement in which Jesus acknowledged the express need for the Holy Ghost to be sent to help interpret what he had said.[6]

It is the Holy Spirit who gives life to the Word. That same Spirit is available for those whose assignment is to create a living experience in those to whom the Word is directed. The incarnation of the Word in the hearts and minds of willing believers is a product first and foremost of God's Spirit. Moreover, as the Holy Spirit was intimately responsible for the incarnation of Jesus Christ in Mary's womb, then so is that same Spirit of God intimately involved in the incarnation of the Word in the lives of the preacher and those to whom he or she preaches. Without that Presence no preaching of the *living* Word can be experienced.

Once the Spirit has been intimately involved in the process of internalizing the Word, the stage is set for creating a *living* experience. Here is the point at which story telling, role playing, and other identification tools become a necessity. The congregation must be able to experience what the text is all about. The Word preached must live before their eyes and in their minds. Nothing should be lost from the preacher's private experience of the Word becoming incarnate in him or her. In fact, the preaching act before a group of listeners should gain even more life and vitality because of the preacher's interaction with other Spirit-filled persons. Again, Dr. Mitchell provides substantiation:

> Congregations quickly visualize and relate to the situation, moving into the experience. The best of biblical scholarship should be used in the development of folksy detail, but it comes alive because it already lives in the teller.[7]

Dr. Mitchell was specifically referring to the eyewitness account experience that facilitates the congregation's visualizing and relating to the text. A good example would be a verbal portrayal of Jacob wrestling with an angel and the resulting limp with which he lived for the rest of his days. The preacher might even limp around the pulpit momentarily to create this experience based on an eyewitness account. Bishop Joseph

A. Johnson, also, provides support for this second step:

> In the heart and mind of the Black preacher through identification, role-playing, translation, commentary and language, that is "preaching language" and voice, the Black preacher has been able to make Scripture come alive and speak to Black congregations, God's Word of healing, peace, liberation and victory.[8]

In the following chapters, the subjects of language and voice will be discussed. These are essential elements of hermeneutics in preaching and enhance the probability of the preacher's creating an experience with the Word among his or her audience.

Creating an experience means that the sermon must become a "happening." It must be a "live" performance, not the "same ole text preached the same ole way." The hearer must become a part of the experiences depicted in the text. Thus, as the biblical character is faced with an experience through which he or she must victoriously come with God's help, the hearer must live through that experience whether it be a shipwreck, a flood, a conversation with a serpent, a hillside sermon, a blessing, a reward, or a cross. In an unpublished lecture, Dr. J. Deotis Roberts cites the late Dr. Martin Luther King, Jr., as one who was extremely successful in creating a living experience among those who heard him preach.

> King's guiding concept, according to Marbury, was that Scripture should be interpreted in such a way that the past becomes alive and illumines our present with new possibilities for personal and social transformation.[9]

Each of these two steps for creating an emotional-intellectual as well as a living experience in those to whom the Word is preached is founded on the fact that people must be able to *relate* to the Word in order to have an experience with it. Thus, an awareness that God is involved in one's holistic liberation and an identification with his Word that speaks to one's existential needs lay the foundation for effective and accurate hermeneutics in preaching, which creates an experience with the Word.

The Evolving Hermeneutical Principle

He or she who interprets and preaches the Word must *allow the Holy Spirit working through his or her gifts and talents to create a living experience with the Word in himself or herself first and then in the lives of those to whom the message is directed.* This is best done through identifying with the Word on an intimate basis via *empathetic application,* eyewitness-account experiences, story telling, and other tools for identification. *Hermeneutical Principle Number Three* involves two essential steps for making the Word incarnate in those to whom the preached Word is delivered: (1) creating an emotional-intellectual experience, and (2) creating a living experience among those to whom the message is directed. All of the preceding is grounded in a theology that promotes the God of liberation who is actively involved in the holistic liberation of all humanity.

Dr. Manuel L. Scott, Sr., expounded upon 2 Corinthians 5:17 and created a living experience with the Word in his contemporary resolution for "the ultimate in urban renewal." Using the familiar formula for church resolutions, Scott proclaimed:

> *Whereas,* the production of new persons (inwardly and outwardly new) cannot be accomplished by any economic system no matter how just and fair; and
> *Whereas,* this production of new persons cannot be achieved by any political ideology, whether communism or capitalism; and
> *Whereas,* the machinery for the making of new men is not available in our empirical and secular educational institutions; and
> *Whereas,* pluralistic ecclesiasticism is progressively rampant, dissipating the energies of religion for the making or for the rebirth of people;
> *Now, therefore, be it resolved* that about the cities, across the nation, and around the world, mankind adopt the Pauline Plan for making new creatures, as mirrored in the fifth chapter and seventeenth verse of Second Corinthians: "Therefore, if any man be in Christ, he is a new creature: old things are passed away; behold, all things are become new."
> *Be it also resolved* that no other collectivity or corporation is an advocate and protagonist of this position except the Christian church.
> *Be it further resolved* that the power of the church to save and socially transform resides in its determination to say and do what is specifically and distinctively Christian. The church's chief resource for reconstruction
> and redemption
> is radicality.
> *Be it finally resolved* that the proposition which the text propagates and pushes has not failed in the experiences of any commonwealth; it simply has not been tried.[10]

Scott's resolution creates a living experience not only for one who hears his message, but also for one who *reads* it; and that is exceptional for published sermons that are read rather than heard.

Another conspicuous example of this hermeneutical principle is found in Scott's sermon, entitled "Unbrotherly Brothers," based on Exodus 2:13. Observe Scott as he creatively and artistically sets the stage for a meaningful experience with this Word in the sermon excerpt quoted previously:

> The opening act in the story
> mirrors that Moses
> did not allow his personal blessings

      to blind him to the burden of his brethren.
Affluence,
    academics,
      and aristocracy
    did not alienate his affection
      nor strangle stimulating concern
        for the less fortunate members of his race.
In spite of his place in Pharaoh's palace and profits from the existing power structure, he initiated and established contact with his Hebrew fellows.
      He took time and effort to see their plight and know their predicament.[11]

Even though the preceding portrayal of Moses is not rendered in the first person, it does allow the listener to utilize *empathetic application* as the preacher gives an "eyewitness account" of Moses' liberation from his advantaged status in order to aid his disadvantaged brothers and sisters. Moreover, both of the excerpts from Scott's sermons create an emotional-intellectual experience as they enable the listeners to live through the story as well as relate the message of each to everyday life.

Sandy F. Ray was divinely gifted with the ability to tell the story of a passage in such a way as to create a living experience with the Word. While in seminary I had the rare privilege of working with Dr. Ray in the Cornerstone Church for four years. It was phenomenal to *experience* the hermeneutics in Dr. Ray's preaching as he unfolded the Word of God before his eager congregation. An example of the genius of Sandy Ray's utilization of this third principle follows as he describes the mission of John the Baptist:

    A strange character broke the silence of centuries with the announcement of the approach of the Messiah. When asked of his identity and his credentials, he replied: "I am the voice of one crying in the wilderness. My name is not as important as my message. . . . My mission is to create a climate for him, to cut a small trail in the vast wilderness where his holy feet may tread."[12]

In a sermon, entitled "The Testimony of a Towel," this pulpit giant tells the story of the disciples' desire for power as the close of Jesus' earthly ministry approached:

    They had started angling for positions in the prospective empire. They had been disputing along the way as to who would be the greatest in the kingdom. A lovely lady had approached him with a request that one of her sons would have a seat on the left and the other on the right. She assumed that both of them would be in his cabinet.[13]

Later in the sermon, Ray makes a smooth transition from the third person to the first person:

Jesus said you have been conditioned in the old system that is rank and racket-ridden. The greatest in my kingdom shall be the towel takers. In my kingdom, seats will be won by service. Crowns are made of towels. If there are no towel takers, the spiritual operation will be greatly impaired. Organized religion has an overabundance of rank-happy, seat and status seekers.[14]

In his sermon "To Keep Footing in a Crumbling Culture," Dr. Ray gives an "eyewitness account" of the story in Matthew 7:24-27. He proclaimed:

Jesus speaks of two men who decided to build a house (Matt. 7:24-27). One of the men was a hasty, happy man. He was eager for occupancy. He found architects, contractors, builders, and workers who accepted his "sand" plans. His house was quickly erected. He was enjoying friends and parties while his neighbor was only at the stage of digging his basement.[15]

The three sermons cited above are but an infinitesimal sampling of the richness and vitality of the experience of Sandy Ray's preaching, which lasted for over a half century.

Dr. William A. Jones, Jr., whose church is within walking distance of the Cornerstone Baptist Church, is a prophetic voice in our difficult times. He exemplified *Hermeneutical Principle Number Three* in the already cited sermon "Back-door Divinity." Here he soliloquizes Jesus:

But from His perspective of totality, where "from everlasting to everlasting" He is, I get the impression that He declares, "I had to do it, and I did." "With me," says God, "I came to the world by way of the back door by both choice and constraint. I willed it that way. And my will involves no contradiction between desire and determination. I wanted to and I had to. I wanted to because I had to, and I had to because I wanted to. I willed it that way. My back-door arrival was consonant with My will.[16]

This sermon excerpt certainly promotes the God of liberation and should create the climate for *all* peoples of every race, color, and culture to experience him as the only living, loving, righteous God who "emptied Himself, taking the form of a servant."

Jones uses the conversation between Dives and Lazarus to publicize "The Horrors of Hell," in the following excerpt of a message evolving from Luke 16:23.

Lazarus saw Dives, but Dives never really saw Lazarus. His vision of Lazarus was that of a blur; there was no clear focus. He did not see a person at his gate, but a derelict, a beggar, a bum.[17]

Black preaching has contributed greatly to the vitality of the preached Word in all segments of the Christian community in America because of its story-telling style, which creates a living experience in the preacher and those to whom the Word is being preached. The ability to get into a text and allow the Holy Spirit to cause that Word to become incarnate in the preacher and his or her people has been a quality of distinction in the best of black preaching. This experience has proven intellectually and emotionally satisfying to black *and* white audiences. Little wonder that whenever a preaching seminar or pastors' conference is held on a major scale by a main-line denomination, interdenominational group, or nondenominational gathering a black pulpiteer is scheduled somewhere on the program. He or she is *expected* to create an experience with the Word.

Preaching in a Common Tongue

The preacher must be able to drive a dump truck if he or she wishes to be successful in creating a living experience with the Word. So Sandy F. Ray likened theologians and biblical scholars to bulldozer operators who unearth the "heavy stuff" of theological treatises, church dogmatics, and exegetical explanations and pile it high and deep for those who would dare seek enlightenment from it. On the other hand, the preacher-pastor, according to Dr. Ray, is the dump-truck driver who makes weekly visits to the "pile," which has been posited by the theologians and biblical scholars, in order to transfer and deposit loads of the "heavy stuff" among the congregation on Sunday morning. Furthermore, Dr. Ray consistently alluded to the fact that there was a distinct division of labor inherent in the processes of unearthing and of transferring the "heavy stuff." In fact Dr. Ray pointed out that theologians and biblical scholars need the preacher-pastor because their scholarly expertise inhibits them from being able to *translate* the "heavy stuff" into understandable language in order that the preaching audience can benefit from it. Thus, the dump-truck driving, preacher-pastor was best gifted to translate and deposit the "heavy stuff" in the hearts and minds of those to whom the Word was directed.

The Word can only be identified with and experienced when it can be understood. Preaching, then, must communicate the Word in the common tongue of those to whom the message is directed. Moreover, he or she who is involved in effective and accurate hermeneutics in preaching must not confuse his or her primary assignment with that of the theologians and biblical scholars. The preacher must be an effective translator of the Word of God or else his or her mission will be defeated immediately after the text is read.

It is also important that the preacher who seeks to translate the Word of God be certain that he or she *first* understands that Word. The interpreter-proclaimer must have a working knowledge of what one has called "language of origination." This prerequisite understanding of the Word to be preached comes through inspired intuition, disciplined Bible study, and basic exegetical skills, all of which enlighten the preacher on the message inherent in the Word. Once this understanding takes place, translation of the Word into the common tongue can begin properly.

In this chapter, the matters of preaching as translation, the dangers of language-out-of-context, and the results of preaching in the common tongue will be highlighted in hopes of arriving at an evolving hermeneutical principle.

Preaching as Translation

Preaching as translation involves the deciphering of the Word in such a way that its message may be clearly proclaimed in familiar and understandable language to those to whom it is directed. Preaching as translation encompasses the process of changing an ancient Word into a contemporary Word that will be heard in the particular idiom of the particular group that receives it. The translation aspect of preaching necessitates interpretation, clarity, change, and cultural awareness and sensitivity. Preaching as translation is all about putting into the words and images of our people the Word of God. In this sense, the preacher must become "bilingual," as he or she involves himself or herself in effective and accurate hermeneutics in preaching. The common tongue of the people to whom the Word is directed ought to be the primary language to which God's Word is translated for those particular people. A primary example is black preaching.

Black preaching has been, and still is, effective and vital in our contemporary times because it has addressed black people in their own language with which they are most familiar and comfortable. (The message has not always been comfortable, mind you, but the *language* has been.) The black preacher has most often realized that one of his or her main tasks is that of translating the Word into the common language of his or her people. If the black preacher was not sensitive and effective in accomplishing this task, then he or she was virtually out of a job. Henry Mitchell suggests: "The best of Black preachers today still know intuitively that they have no allegiance to any cultural criteria save the idiom of the people."[1]

It has also been pointed out by Dr. Mitchell that the most effective preaching in the black church community as well as in the broader Christian community occurs when the preacher successfully creates the climate in which his or her listeners can identify with the *words* as well as the Word being proclaimed. Mitchell writes:

> It is also vital that preachers often identify linguistically with the *real* congregants, *all* of them, as opposed to the persons they seek to be, even though the preacher may also be a model of their upward goal.[2]

In recent years many black preachers have had the opportunity to attend colleges and seminaries in preparation for their pastoral ministries. With this exposure to theological institutions of higher learning has come the necessity to learn and acquire another language uncommon in form (but not in substance) with the language of those to whom most of their preaching will be directed. The language to which I have reference is the primarily cerebral and abstract vernacular of white Anglo-Saxon Protestant theologians and biblical scholars.

However impressive the theological jargon of the classic and contemporary theological guilds is, the truth that needs to be conveyed through the Word must be posited before the people in an understandable tongue. The majority of the constituents—white or black—who hear the Word preached are *not* familiar with the theological language prevalent on campuses and in lectures and writings emanating from institutions of higher theological learning. Therefore, to preach the Word of God in such a language before one's people would be hardly different from the "glossolalian controversy" addressed by the apostle Paul in 1 Corinthians 14:2-14. To this end writes Dr. Mitchell: "Black preaching is as effective as it is in the Black community because it has never tried to wage a major war against the culture of the masses of folk."[3] In the concluding section of this chapter, the preaching of the three noted black preachers will be cited to further substantiate the contribution of the black preaching tradition in this area.

The danger of using language out of context ought to be recognized by any person engaged in the interpretation and proclamation of the Word. That is what I call "mismatched preaching language." This unfortunate combination consists of the Word of God being interpreted in a language *other* than the language of those to whom the message is directed. Moreover, this danger does not refer only to theological language being preached before a black congregation. It confronts any "mismatched preaching language" and people. In his book *Black Belief*, Mitchell suggests that the effectiveness of the black preacher has a lot to do with the fact that he or she does not attempt to give his or her people a vocabulary lesson in conjunction with his or her message on Sunday morning. In his exact words, Dr. Mitchell said: "The professionally educated Black preacher . . . will translate his most sophisticated insights into the folk idiom and imagery of their culture, *not vice versa* [italics added]."[4] Any attempt to do otherwise merely alienates and confuses the recipients of "mismatched preaching language" and, at the most, vainly impresses the hearers of the language out of context. Identification with the Word cannot take place under these circumstances by a majority of those present.

I was rudely awakened to the danger of language out of context when I was studying religion and philosophy at Bishop College in Dallas, Texas. One of the local pastors annually sponsored a youth revival, affording several of the student ministers an opportunity to preach before a "live" congregation. Providentially, I was asked to preach one night. The sermon ended successfully in my opinion. However, due to my zealousness to share with that "*un*enlightened" black congregation my recently acquired knowledge, I bulldozed a load or two of egotistically oriented verbiage that included phrases like "the caliginosity of blinding opacity caused by sorrow and self-pity" and "the nigritude of transgressive darkness." After the message, the kind pastor came to me outside of the church and said, "Son, I didn't know you had such a good mind. But you lost my folks! Now, you came back and picked them up at the end, but for a good while you lost my folks. You probably don't like what I'm saying to you, *but don't lose the folk!"*

"Don't lose the folk" should be a watchword by which all who interpret and preach the Word of God should guard themselves from "mismatched preaching language." Since my conversation with that pastor, I have been in the business of translating the Word preached into the common language of those to whom the message is directed. Again, Paul, one of the most gifted preachers in the history of the church, substantiates this concern for clarity in the pulpit: "For God is not a God of [linguistic] confusion but of peace" (1 Corinthians 14:33).

The Results of Preaching in the Common Tongue

Powerful preaching is one of the results of preaching in the common tongue of those to whom one's message is directed. Since one definition of power is "authority given to another by a person or group," it follows then that the preacher whose hermeneutics are effective in translating the Word of God will be granted rightful influence as a proclaimer of the gospel by his or her audience. Martin Luther King, Jr., Billy Graham, Edward V. Hill, and many other noted pulpiteers of this era have all been recipients of enormous and far-reaching power, due in part to their ability to translate. The same also is evident in the local church when the preacher-pastor takes very seriously the objective of preaching in the common language of those who will hear his or her message. In essence, the words heard by the congregation are God's Word translated into *their* words. The most perfect example of this consequence of *preaching as translation* is the dynamic message of Jesus Christ, of which one exclaimed, "No man ever spoke like this man!" (John 7:46).

To have one's preaching remembered is a second by-product of preaching in the language of the people. *Preaching as translation* is usually memorable preaching. It is memorable because persons are allowed to experience the Word in understandable terms, symbols, and images. Moreover, common, everyday language in preaching makes for *portable* preaching, preaching that can be carried home. The thoughts and ideas presented by the preacher are easily transported to the hearts and minds of the listeners and, eventually, to their everyday lives. Therefore, one of the most important evaluative comments which a parishioner can make to a preacher-pastor does not address the profundity of the preacher's vocabulary, but the *understandability* of what has been said. Once understanding takes place, remembering the preached Word becomes much easier. The two-thousand-year-old preaching of the Prophet from Nazareth bears out this point on memorable preaching. It is the hope of any of us who preach the Gospel to have at least some thing we say at the eleven o'clock hour on Sunday remembered at noonday on Monday.

The Evolving Hermeneutical Principle

He or she who interprets and preaches the Word must *proclaim the Word in the common tongue of the majority of those who will hear his or her message on any given occasion.* This principle involves translating the Word of God and its truth into the particular idiom of the particular group to whom the message is directed. When this principle is practiced, the danger of preaching in a language out of context and/ or mismatched preaching language is virtually eliminated. It results in powerful and memorable preaching because it creates the climate whereby the listeners can relate to the vocabulary of the message as well as the Word. In addition, it is patterned after the preaching of Jesus.

Dr. Manuel L. Scott, Sr., is gifted with a noble command of the king's English. There have been occasions when Dr. Scott has been accused of writing in a language uncommon to his own people. His first book, *From a Black Brother,* has been the primary evidence supporting that criticism. As a matter of fact, Dr. Scott says that his first book was an effort to help bridge the gap between Southern Baptists and Negro Baptists. This is not to say that Scott's initial book was written in the common language of Southern Baptists. Nevertheless, in a message in that book dealing with "the temptations of the Negro preaching community," Dr. Scott prophetically denounced the highly visible charades of a segment of the "Black preaching fraternity" in relatively translatable language:

> Even a casual observer knows that we have far too many Negro Baptist preachers who bombastically brag and bark, who are exhibitive and extravagant, frothy and fanfaronadish, grandiloquent and gallery players, ostentatious and obtruse, playboyish and publicity stunters, and who splash and splurge.[5]

In the paragraph below, based on Exodus 2:13, Scott translates the thoughts of Moses after he sees two of his Hebrew brothers in conflict with one another:

> Ponder a paraphrase of Moses' perception when he raises the question we are considering: To the two men who are tangling, Moses really is saying: Striking your fellow does not make sense. Both of you are Hebrews. Both of you have a common history in hardship. Both of you are slaves in the Egyptian empire. Both of you are bossed and bought. Both of you are victims of organized and systemic evil. It seems to me that your common circumstances should goad you into some alliance and excite you to cohesion rather than to competition and conflict.[6]

There is no way that any members of the adult black community could miss the message of these words.

Though William A. Jones, Jr., is another leading pulpiteer who utilizes a wide vocabulary to his advantage, his preaching yet involves *preaching as translation*. In his message "In Flesh for Flesh," Jones put into the common tongue of his constituents of the ghetto God's concern for them. He preached:

> He's interested in slums and suburbs, preachers and politicians, the needy and the greedy. God's concerned about alleys and avenues, jet planes and jails, sinners and saints. God is upset over nuclear nonsense, political corruption, starvation, malnutrition, economic exploitation, and racial injustice.[7]

Jones, in communicating with his audience about the condition of Lazarus' earthly life, said, "His earthly existence was marked by dreadful poverty. He was a welfare recipient in the most degrading manner."[8]

Putting the preached Word into the language of the majority of those to whom he preached was one of the most memorable aspects of the preaching of Sandy F. Ray. Doctors and lawyers, politicians and poor people, professionals, and those on fixed incomes heard him gladly. In a sermon entitled "To Keep Footing in a Crumbling Culture," Dr. Ray proclaimed:

One may lose footing by an awkward step. Numerous people in this world are suffering with a handicapping limp as the result of an awkward step. There are "watch-your-step" cautions all about us. . . . Parents, teachers, preachers, and the Bible are striving to shield careless, indiscreet, remiss people from stumbling.[9]

Dealing with singing "melodies in a strange land," Ray moves his audience to identify with the circumstances of our enslaved foreparents by using these words:

"How shall we sing?" We have symphonic souls. We have chirping, chanting spirits. We are on a rhythmic mission. Singing and praising God cheer us along the weary way. We sing in strange lands, difficult situations, and horrible conditions. . . .

Our songs may not be suited to a choir or a professional chorus. They may not be in a church or a temple. They may be in a lonely apartment, basement, on a farm, in a factory, a hospital room, an office, in the air, on land, or on sea. The soul has a song for all of life's situations.[10]

In speaking about visionaries and dreamers, based on Joseph who was cast into a hole by his jealous brothers, Sandy Ray translated into everyday language the lesson from Joseph's experience:

Dreamers must be cautious about where and to whom they tell their dreams. It is disconcerting to tell dreams which we cannot sell. . . . Nondreamers do not buy dreams quickly. Good leaders learn to drop dreams as they prepare the market to sell them. Young preachers must observe this carefully and prayerfully. Do not marshal dreams out too early. It is a waste in a dreamless society.[11]

Preaching in the common tongue of those who will receive the Word leads to their edification as well as inspiration. If it is indeed the preacher's lot to communicate to the world that God is actively involved in its holistic liberation, then preaching must be done in a language that can be understood by any particular group to whom the message is directed at any given time. The Word that the preacher must proclaim is too vital and vivacious for its life to be stymied by egotistical verbosity or linguistic insensitivity. As alluded to in Sandy Ray's illustration that began this chapter, the preacher, and especially the preacher-pastor, must recognize his or her primary responsibility as translator. Then and only then can the Word be powerfully and memorably communicated to the people in a common tongue.

Proclaiming the Word

Hermeneutics in preaching is *unfinished* until the living Word is effectively proclaimed as the spoken Word. The culminating act of the hermeneutical process involves "getting the Word off the paper." Preaching has always been an oral exercise. One can effectively and accurately move through the hermeneutical steps previously mentioned and still fail in communicating the Word if the proclamation event is not perceived as a necessary step by the preacher. Proclaiming the Word must be conclusive in its effect upon people. On this matter, Carl E. Braaten comments: "Preaching today is the goal of exegesis and hermeneutical reflection. The oral character of the Word is decisive. The Word is an 'acoustical event.'"[1]

In this chapter, the matters of preaching as dialogue, communicating the Word interpretively, and concluding the spoken Word will be discussed in an effort to identify a final hermeneutical principle.

Preaching as Dialogue

Preaching as dialogue suggests that the proclamation of the spoken Word is a conversation between the preacher and his or her congregation. The Word was never meant to be read only—quite the contrary! Biblical scholars inform us that the written words of various personalities in the Bible were inscribed long after they had been spoken and were written to be read aloud in public. The Word to be proclaimed is not only an "acoustical event," as Braaten has written, but also a public event.

The Word that has been received, deciphered, and translated into the common language of the people is to be shared horizontally in dialogue with those to whom the message is directed. In using the word "horizontally," emphasis is meant to be placed on dialogue that is on the same level as the people. Preaching as dialogue significantly recognizes the presence of persons and their interaction with the Word. When the Word is being proclaimed, it is not to be an act of condescension. That was done when the Word became flesh. The preacher must engage in horizontal dialogue that reaches the heart and mind of each of his or her listeners.

Preaching as dialogue dictates that hermeneutics in preaching should be participatory. Because preaching is at once acoustical, public, and horizontal in proclamation, those who listen are participants in the hermeneutical process. Henry Mitchell, in *The Recovery of Preaching*, highlights this point in these words, "To achieve vital experience with transconscious impact, preaching demands participation. Proclamation with power requires dialogue." [2] It is for this reason that *Hermeneutical Principle Number Two* is so important. When persons can relate to the *content* of the message through identification with the Word, they are more apt to identify with and participate in the acoustical event.

For example, in many black congregations today it takes more than an acoustical event to engage the congregants in participation with the preached Word. People initially respond to the sound of a preacher's voice, but that is only temporary. Once they plug into his or her voice, they must be able to identify with and experience the Word. If the experience with the Word does not take place, the quality of the voice can be virtually written off, along with the sermon.

Participation by the audience insures the preacher that dialogue is occurring. The issue is not necessarily *how* the audience participates, because various congregations within the same cultural group may express their participation in a multitude of ways, depending upon the occasion, the message, and the preacher. Dr. Mitchell further explains:

> The word dialogue is used here to denote the pulpit/pew context of spontaneous interaction, which may be audible or silent—involving physical or body language and/or mental response. Whatever the form, the communicating and responding are genuine. [3]

The main point is that "getting the Word off the paper" entails engaging the audience in dialogue with the preacher. Preaching as dialogue, then, acknowledges the presence of persons and invites them to participate in the culminating act of hermeneutics in preaching.

The black preaching tradition has made a significant contribution to the Christian community in this area. There is probably no other context in the United States of America in which preaching as dialogue has been so evident, vital, and authentic as in the black church. Monologue is hardly the order of the day in the black experience in religion. In addition, the participatory character of black worship permeates more than the preached Word. There is a rumor about a certain church in an

Atlantic seaboard city which purports that the parishioners are known to shout when the announcements and hymn numbers are read aloud. Whatever the case, participation through dialogue is par for the course when it comes to black preaching. Bishop Johnson in discussing hermeneutics describes black preaching's contributions in this area:

> The uniqueness of Black preaching is determined by the context in which it takes place. The Black preacher's style which included the pattern of call and response—a dialogue between preacher and congregation, are, if you please, a trilogy in which the Holy Spirit moves the Black preacher, and the Black preacher speaks to the congregation and the congregation responds with, "Amen," "That's Right," "Tell it like it is," "Go ahead Son," "Let the Spirit have its way," . . . what takes place in the true Black worship is not superstition, but rather a real, natural dialogue.[4]

Oral tradition is another factor that has kept preaching as dialogue alive and well in the black church. The African roots that are extant in most American blacks include a strong link to oral tradition. Deprived for so long of the right to learn to read, the slaves enhanced their ability to retain that which they heard and repeated aloud to others the same message. They were forced, for survival reasons, to overcome their literacy restraints and, as a result, used the genius of oral tradition to keep alive by remembrance that which was important. The tablets of mind and heart are, after all, the ultimate repository.

A case in point is my grandfather, who died at the age of seventy-nine in 1977. Three months before he died, one of the deacons of the First Institutional Baptist Church interviewed him on tape. During the course of the conversation, my grandfather, Clarence S. Washington, Sr., was asked about his "roots." To my utter amazement, my grandfather revealed for the first time ever that his father, who was a freed slave living in Oklahoma, was not originally named Washington. He went on to explain that his father was approached by bounty hunters looking for fugitive slaves, and when asked his name, he replied, "George, ah, George Washington," rather than his real name, which was George Robinson. It had never been mentioned or written down anywhere that the family name was really Robinson rather than the name by which my grandfather and his eleven children have been known. Only under a condition in which authentic dialogue took place was this significant bit of family history orally communicated.

The contribution of oral tradition helps to explain the key role that preaching as dialogue has played in the black church. Things happen when the written Word is proclaimed from a black pulpit! The participation by the preacher *and* the pew causes a dynamism and creative atmosphere that is not apparent in many other Christian communities.

The Word lives on the level of the people as they participate in the sacred conversation that God's Word through the preacher is having with them. Dr. Henry Mitchell comments on one consequence of this experience:

> The traditional Black pulpit thus radiates influence because of its folk interpretation of the Bible, which was itself originally a folk document, and because that folk interpretation is, like all authentic folk materials, relevant and lively.[5]

Influence in the pulpit is waiting for the preacher who would dare to dialogue with his or her people rather than monologue.

Communicating the Word Interpretively

The effective preacher must be an oral interpreter as well as an insightful and studious hermeneutical practitioner. The spoken Word requires "hermeneutics on the feet" in addition to that which is done in the sermon preparation room. The voice and body of the preacher are to be utilized in communicating the Word interpretively. I would not dare to estimate how many thousands of excellently prepared sermons have been sacrificed unnecessarily because the proclaimer had little or no knowledge and skill as an oral interpreter.

I was made aware of the necessity to communicate the Word interpretively while taking a course in the communications department of the Arizona State University. The course was entitled "Interpretation as Literary Criticism." It was during this course that I realized that the hermeneutical process continues while the spoken Word is being preached. Moreover, the more skilled and knowledgeable one is in oral interpretation, the more effective and meaningful one's oral presentation will become. Consequently, I concluded that if oral interpretation works on performances of written materials by authors such as Frederich Nietzsche, Sarah Ann Dupee, and Vachel Lindsay, then it can certainly work on the Word of God that was meant to be spoken.

A manual written by Drs. Kristen B. Valentine and D. E. Valentine, entitled *Interlocking Pieces,* highlights the relationship of communication and interpretation as follows:

> The process of communicating literature is an *act* by someone wishing to say something to someone. . . . Experiencing literature as an act implies a dynamic, rather than a passive, relationship between the interpreter, the literature, and the audience. Literature is more fully comprehended when it is communicated; and when comprehension is continually being worked on, the communication is more effective. The more thoroughly the interpreter understands a work of literature, the better s/he will interpret it aloud; the more the work is interpreted aloud, the better the understanding.[6]

The preceding statement directly relates to the hermeneutical principles already discussed in chapters 2 and 3, specifically, the process of identifying with and experiencing the Word by both the preacher and the audience. And it goes a step further to emphasize the interpreting aloud of the spoken literature, which in turn leads to better understanding by the speaker and the audience.

Communicating the Word interpretively involves, first of all, the preacher-interpreter's becoming intimate with the Word that is to be preached. He or she must know and understand the message that shall be proclaimed before the waiting congregation. To become intimate with one's preaching material requires time and solitude (for most). The next step entails reading the message *aloud* to oneself, oftentimes, over and over and over again. Then, and only then, will the preacher get an opportunity to *hear* the Word that others will eventually hear. A third step includes the process of empathetic application. The preacher needs to know the various feelings of the Word to be preached—the moments of low intensity and high intensity, expressions of exhilaration, melancholy, encouragement, and conviction. Once he or she knows the various feelings prompted by the Word, the succeeding step is that of expressing the feelings through voice inflections and volume, body gestures, facial expressions, and constant eye contact. The rhythm and pacing of one's message are also key factors in continuing an effective hermeneutical process while on one's feet. Dr. Mitchell reminds the preacher to *"Give people adequate time to relate transconsciously, or in depth, to every significant idea of meaning presented."* [7]

All of the above is involved in communicating the Word *interpretively* which, in turn, gives direction to the preacher's oral hermeneutical process.

Effective and accurate hermeneutics in preaching has the final purpose of causing persons to *do*—either to do better, do less, do more, or do differently. Henry Mitchell places a great degree of emphasis on preaching as celebration in his book *The Recovery of Preaching.*[8] He writes about concluding a sermon in these words:

> The final role of celebration is that fitting climax to a balanced proclamation which has already included exegesis, exposition, explanation, application, and deeply meaningful illustration. The gospel should have been proclaimed throughout with joy.[9]

In most situations this is absolutely true. However, intertwined with celebration must be challenge to the hearers. Those who hear the preached Word must be simultaneously lifted to creative celebrative heights and challenged to allow themselves to be liberated to become all that God has designed them to become. One's hermeneutics must have the intent of creating an experience whereby people can hear the Word gladly and be healed and made whole. Understandably, there is no set way to conclude every sermon to accomplish this two-fold purpose. Some of the best advice comes from Bishop Joseph A. Johnson's late father, "Remember your planned or anticipated climax in the sermon may not be God's climax for that sermon." [10] Being in tune with the Spirit as well as sensing the need and mood of one's audience will, no doubt, inform one on how the message should conclude.

The Evolving Hermeneutical Principle

He or she who interprets and preaches the Word must *proclaim the Word as dialogue with the audience and utilize the voice and body to communicate interpretively one's message and its meaning.* This principle acknowledges the presence of the members of the audience who are simultaneously engaged in interpreting the spoken Word. It fosters their participation in the preaching event. The interpretive aspect of this principle recognizes preaching as essentially an oral event. Therefore, one who preaches must acquire and enhance skills that enable him or her to become an effective oral interpreter and to ground his or her messages in solid exegesis and hermeneutics. This principle, when effectively demonstrated in the preaching event, culminates in the climax that creates an atmosphere for celebration and challenges the audience to act according to the preached Word.

Documenting on paper preaching as dialogue and the spoken Word communicated interpretively presents some problems. The problems merely accentuate the importance of *Hermeneutical Principle Number Five* for the preacher. The only suggestion this writer has at this point is for the reader of this book to read aloud the examples of this principle.

William A. Jones, Jr., has a way of using his resounding baritone voice, coupled with indigenous rhythm, to proclaim powerfully the Word interpretively. In the following excerpt, he exemplifies this skill as he converses with his audience about "Back-door Divinity." Listen to Jones proclaim:

> Lastly, He came by way of the back door because that's the location of most of His children. It is not my purpose to deal with the thorny issue of social disparity. My main concern is to lift up the truth about God's concern for the whole of humanity, and the unalterable, undeniable reality is that most of His children are back-door dwellers. I have touched down on every continent under heaven. I've felt the bitter winds of the Arctic, the chill of a Russian winter, and the warm zephyrs of West Africa. I've sailed Victoria Harbor in the Crown Colony of Hong Kong, and I've gone by steamer along the Rhine through the lush vineyards of West Germany. I've walked the streets of London and viewed the white cliffs of Dover.

. . . I've traveled America from top to bottom and from coast to coast. And everywhere, throughout my Father's world, most of His children are back-door dwellers. Many are hungry and dying of malnutrition. Many are crying for a taste of freedom. Some are living fairly well, but struggling to hold on to what they have. And all of them sing the lament, "I'm rolling thru an unfriendly world." [11]

If one reads this with intimacy and feeling, one can get an idea of the effectiveness of Jones' preaching in utilizing this principle.

In a message entitled "The Beasts and the Angels," Jones verbally paints a picture of the scene at Jesus' baptism by John. Feel the atmosphere Jones creates with these words:

Jubilance filled the sky, excitement rode on the wings of the passing breeze, the Spirit descended like a dove, and a voice spoke from the other side of existence, saying, "This is my beloved Son, in whom I am well pleased" (Mt. 3:17). What a morning it must have been! The sky cleft asunder, the Spirit come down, God speaking! [12]

Sandy Ray was a master in preaching as dialogue. He utilized very few body gestures and voice inflections. However, his art of pacing himself and interjecting well-placed pauses following major points in his sermons has been matched by few pulpiteers in this generation. I watched Dr. Ray preach numbers of sermons without observing him exert an enormous amount of wasted physical energy. In fact I saw him hardly ever moving from behind the podium. He could simply "talk" people into participating in the spoken Word. In the following lines, he talks about people's desire to acquire things the easy way:

Escalators give us a more comfortable and easy lift upward, but the stairway gives more effort and stamina. More people have been escalated to levels of success but have never experienced the stairway struggles. Instant success, escalated power, and privileges can become dangerous and disastrous.

Jesus speaks of two men who decided to build a house (Matt. 7:24-27). One of the men was a hasty, happy man. He was eager for occupancy. He found architects, contractors, builders, and workers who accepted his "sand" plans. His house was quickly erected. He was enjoying friends and parties while his neighbor was only at the stage of digging his basement. [13]

Dr. Ray engages his audience in the following dialogue as Jesus gives the disciples their job description when he was preparing to return to his Father:

Jesus sensed their ambitions for power. He said, "Ye shall receive power, after that the Holy Ghost is come upon you" (Acts 1:8). This power will not be military or economic or political. You will not have titles of office. "Ye shall be witnesses." You shall have a testimony.

Testimonies are more important than titles. A title is a rank, office, or an attainment bestowed by people. These titles and offices may be cancelled by the act of people.[14]

Manuel Scott, Sr., is known not only for his powerful message but also for his unique and attractive pulpit gestures. He is one who needs to be *seen* as well as heard. It is more difficult to exemplify the principle outlined in this chapter with Scott's preaching than with Ray's or Jones's. Nevertheless, an attempt will be made.

In his message "Recipe for Racial Greatness," Scott proclaims:

Without apology or ambiguity, they affirmed to Joshua: "We are a great people."
This was another way of saying that they liked themselves.
They could be themselves without being ashamed.
They were not inclined to mimic, mindlessly, other people.
They had a sense of being somebody. . . .
They were not cringing and
          crawling and
                    bowing and
                              blushing
before anyone.[15]

Concluding his message in celebration and challenge is most often an ecstatic experience for Scott and his audience. The climax of his sermon based on 2 Corinthians 5:17 is an example.

Consider in conclusion that the text makes it diamondly clear that it is only in Christ that a new man comes to be.
One is not made new simply by making a studious perusal of the Bible.
One is not made new by sheer subscription to Christian morality.
One is not made new by altruism and humanitarianism.
One is not made new by holding citizenship in a predominantly Christian culture.
One is not made new by the pronouncements of religious prelates, potentates, presbyteries, pastors, and preachers.
One is not made new by being tied to a particular family tree.
One is not made new by having membership in the organized Christian church, though he is regular in his attendance and faithful in the discharge of his visible and vocal duties. . . .
To be most truly Christian, one must be in Christ.[16]

My best advice to a reader of this book is to purchase an available tape recording or record album of either of these three preaching giants. One would have to hear Sandy Ray utilize his conversational tone of voice, timely pauses, and plain-spoken celebrative conclusions really to appreciate his "hermeneutics on the feet." William Jones would have to be seen and heard in person in order for one to value his interpretive facial expressions, methodical sermon building, suggestive voice inflections, and crescendoing climax. Manuel Scott, with his unusual head gyrations, intense rubbing of his forehead, emphatic voice gurgling at the conclusion of important statements, and even his occasional suspender-popping communicates with an audiovisual interpretation of God's Word for those who are present when he preaches. It would do one well to experience the Word preached by Scott and Jones in a "live" setting. Regardless of the setting, it will become obvious that their preaching is meant to be heard and is best understood that way.

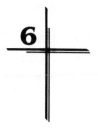

6

Summary

In the preceding pages, I have identified evolving hermeneutical principles and ideas that are evident in black preaching at its best. This was done not merely to accentuate the interpretive process that has been involved in black preaching since antebellum days but also to illustrate the significant contribution that hermeneutics in black preaching can make to all who preach the Word of God.

Let us review the five basic hermeneutical principles that are a product of this study.

Hermeneutical Principle Number One

He or she who interprets and preaches the Word must *know God to be actively involved in the continuous process of humankind's holistic liberation.*

Hermeneutical Principle Number Two

He or she who interprets and preaches the Word must *identify with the Word in such a way that the Word will both support and challenge those to whom the message is directed.*

Hermeneutical Principle Number Three

He or she who interprets and preaches the Word must *allow the Holy Spirit working through his or her gifts and talents to create a living experience with the Word in himself or herself first, and then in the lives of those to whom the message is directed.*

Hermeneutical Principle Number Four

He or she who interprets and preaches the Word must *proclaim the Word in the common tongue of the majority of those who will hear his or her message on any given occasion.*

Hermeneutical Principle Number Five

He or she who interprets and preaches the Word must *proclaim the Word as dialogue with the audience and utilize the voice and body to communicate interpretively one's message and its meaning.*

When these hermeneutical principles are coupled with sound exegetical homework, one should be able to preach the Word effectively and accurately in any context, the end result being preaching that is relevant and understandable. This, then, would enable the preacher to accomplish the directive initially given by the apostle Paul to his son in the ministry, Timothy, and found in 2 Timothy 2:15: "Do your best to present yourself to God as one approved, a workman who has no need to be ashamed, rightly handling the word of truth." "Rightly handling the word of truth" is the primary responsibility of all of us who preach. That is what hermeneutics in preaching is all about. Therefore, hermeneutics *is* an essential tool for telling the Story.

Footnotes

Chapter 1

[1] Joseph A. Johnson, *Proclamation Theology* (Shreveport, La.: Fourth Episcopal District Press, 1977), p. 35.

[2] J. Deotis Roberts, *A Black Political Theology* (Philadelphia: The Westminster Press, 1974), pp. 112-113. Copyright © 1974 The Westminster Press. Used by permission.

[3] Johnson, *Proclamation Theology*, pp. 38-39.

[4] Henry H. Mitchell, *The Recovery of Preaching* (New York: Harper & Row Publishers, Inc., 1977), p. 17. Copyright © 1977 by Henry H. Mitchell. By permission of Harper & Row, Publishers, Inc.

[5] J. Deotis Roberts, "The Hermeneutic Circle of Black Theology" (an unpublished article written in Summer 1980), p. 2.

[6] *Ibid.*, p. 35.

[7] Johnson, *Proclamation Theology*, p. 50.

[8] James H. Cone, *A Black Theology of Liberation* (Philadelphia: J. B. Lippincott Co., 1970), p. 115.

[9] Sandy F. Ray, *Journeying Through a Jungle* (Nashville: Broadman Press, 1979), pp. 89-90. All rights reserved. Used by permission.

[10] Manuel L. Scott, *From a Black Brother* (Nashville: Broadman Press, 1973), p. 108.

[11] *Ibid.*, p. 110.

[12] William A. Jones, Jr., "God and the Ghetto," *God in the Ghetto* (Elgin, Ill.: Progressive Baptist Publishing House, 1979), p. 67. Used by permission.

[13] Jones, "Back-door Divinity," *God in the Ghetto*, p. 124.

[14] Manuel L. Scott, "Cross Power," *The Gospel for the Ghetto* (Nashville: Broadman Press, 1973), pp. 65-66.

[15] Scott, "Biblical Basis for Brotherhood," *The Gospel for the Ghetto*, p. 108.

[16] Ray, "To Keep Footing in a Crumbling Culture," *Journeying*, p. 52.

[17] Jones, "God and the Ghetto," *God in the Ghetto*, p. 68.

[18] Jones, "The Beasts and the Angels," *God in the Ghetto*, p. 135.

[19] Jones, "In Flesh for Flesh," *God in the Ghetto*, p. 131.

Chapter 2

[1] Richard R. Rohrbaugh, *The Biblical Interpreter* (Philadelphia: Fortress Press, 1978), p. 23.

[2] J. Deotis Roberts, *A Black Political Theology* (Philadelphia: The Westminster Press, 1974), p. 127.

[3] J. Deotis Roberts, "The Hermeneutic Circle of Black Theology" (an unpublished article written in Summer 1980), pp. 8-9.

⁴Henry H. Mitchell, *The Recovery of Preaching* (New York: Harper & Row Publishers, Inc., 1977), p. 30.

⁵Joseph A. Johnson, *Proclamation Theology* (Shreveport, La.: Fourth Episcopal District Press, 1977), p. 50.

⁶*Ibid.*, p. 45.

⁷Mitchell, *The Recovery of Preaching*, p. 38.

⁸*Ibid.*, pp. 83-84.

⁹Johnson, *Proclamation Theology*, p. 50.

¹⁰Rohrbaugh, *The Biblical Interpreter*, p. 17.

¹¹James A. Sanders, *God Has a Story Too* (Philadelphia: Fortress Press, 1979), p. 5.

¹²James A. Sanders, "Hermeneutics," *The Interpreter's Dictionary of the Bible*, supplementary volume (Nashville: Abingdon Press, 1976), p. 406.

¹³Sanders, *God Has a Story Too*, p. 22.

¹⁴Sanders, "Hermeneutics," p. 405.

¹⁵James A. Sanders, "Jeremiah and the Future of Theological Scholarship," *Andover Newton Quarterly*, 13 (1972), p. 133.

¹⁶Sanders, *God Has a Story Too*, p. 20.

¹⁷William A. Jones, Jr., "Back-door Divinity," *God in the Ghetto* (Elgin, Ill.: Progressive Baptist Publishing House, 1979), p. 122.

¹⁸*Ibid.*, p. 123.

¹⁹*Ibid.*, p. 124.

²⁰Jones, "In Flesh for Flesh," *God in the Ghetto*, p. 127.

²¹*Ibid.*, p. 130.

²²Jones, "On Prophets and Potentates," *God in the Ghetto*, p. 152.

²³*Ibid.*

²⁴Manuel L. Scott, *From a Black Brother* (Nashville: Broadman Press, 1971), p. 14.

²⁵*Ibid.*, p. 77.

²⁶*Ibid.*, p. 78.

²⁷Manuel L. Scott, "The Ultimate in Urban Renewal," *The Gospel for the Ghetto* (Nashville: Broadman Press, 1973), p. 24.

²⁸Scott, "Unbrotherly Brothers," *The Gospel for the Ghetto*, p. 73.

²⁹*Ibid.*, p. 75.

³⁰Sandy F. Ray, "Journeying Through a Jungle," *Journeying Through a Jungle* (Nashville: Broadman Press, 1979), pp. 25-26.

³¹Ray, "The Testimony of a Towel," *Journeying*, pp. 35-36.

³²*Ibid.*, p. 38.

³³Ray, "The Challenge of the Wood Country," *Journeying*, p. 79.

³⁴*Ibid.*, p. 81.

³⁵Ray, "Take a Little Honey," *Journeying*, p. 99.

Chapter 3

¹Henry H. Mitchell, *The Recovery of Preaching* (New York: Harper & Row Publishers, Inc., 1977), p. 33.

²*Ibid.*, p. 37.

³Joseph A. Johnson, *Proclamation Theology* (Shreveport, La.: Fourth Episcopal District Press, 1977), p. 48.

⁴*Ibid.*, p. 42.

⁵James H. Cone, *God of the Oppressed* (New York: The Seabury Press, 1975), p. 57.

⁶Mitchell, *The Recovery of Preaching*, p. 90.

⁷*Ibid.*, p. 84.

⁸Johnson, *Proclamation Theology*, p. 48.

⁹J. Deotis Roberts, "The Hermeneutic Circle of Black Theology" (an unpublished article written in Summer 1980), p. 24.

¹⁰Manuel L. Scott, "The Ultimate in Urban Renewal," *The Gospel for the Ghetto* (Nashville: Broadman Press, 1973), pp. 24-25.

¹¹Scott, "Unbrotherly Brothers," *The Gospel for the Ghetto*, p. 75.

[12]Sandy F. Ray, "Journeying Through a Jungle," *Journeying Through a Jungle* (Nashville: Broadman Press, 1979), pp. 23-24.

[13]Ray, "The Testimony of a Towel," *Journeying,* p. 31.

[14]*Ibid.,* p. 34.

[15]Ray, "To Keep Footing in a Crumbling Culture," *Journeying,* p. 50.

[16]William A. Jones, Jr., "Back-door Divinity," *God in the Ghetto* (Elgin, Ill.: Progressive Baptist Publishing House, 1979), p. 121.

[17]Jones, "The Horrors of Hell," *God in the Ghetto,* p. 143.

Chapter 4

[1]Henry H. Mitchell, *Black Preaching* (Philadelphia: J. B. Lippincott Co., 1970), p. 29.

[2]Henry H. Mitchell, *The Recovery of Preaching* (New York: Harper & Row Publishers, Inc., 1977), pp. 100-101.

[3]*Ibid.,* p. 24.

[4]Henry H. Mitchell, *Black Belief* (New York: Harper & Row Publishers, Inc., 1977), p. 13.

[5]Manuel L. Scott, *From a Black Brother* (Nashville: Broadman Press, 1971), p. 80.

[6]Manuel L. Scott, *The Gospel for the Ghetto,* (Nashville: Broadman Press, 1973), pp. 77-78.

[7]William A. Jones, Jr., "In Flesh for Flesh," *God in the Ghetto,* (Elgin, Ill.: Progressive Baptist Publishing House, 1979), p. 131.

[8]Jones, "The Horrors of Hell," *God in the Ghetto,* p. 143.

[9]Sandy F. Ray, "To Keep Footing in a Crumbling Culture," *Journeying Through a Jungle* (Nashville: Broadman Press, 1979), p. 49.

[10]Ray, "Melodies in a Strange Land," *Journeying,* p. 61.

[11]Ray, "Take a Little Honey," *Journeying,* p. 96.

Chapter 5

[1]Carl E. Braaten, *New Directions in Theology Today, Vol. II History and Hermeneutics* (Philadelphia: The Westminster Press, 1974), p. 138.

[2]Henry H. Mitchell, *The Recovery of Preaching* (New York: Harper & Row Publishers, Inc., 1970), p. 115.

[3]*Ibid.,* p. 116.

[4]Joseph A. Johnson, *Proclamation Theology* (Shreveport, La.: Fourth Episcopal District Press, 1977), p. 41.

[5]Mitchell, *The Recovery of Preaching,* p. 83.

[6]Kristen B. and D. E. Valentine, *Interlocking Pieces,* second edition (Dubuque, Iowa: Kendall/Hunt Publishing Co., 1980), p. vii.

[7]Mitchell, *The Recovery of Preaching,* p. 43.

[8]*Ibid.,* pp. 54-73.

[9]*Ibid.,* p. 58.

[10]Johnson, *Proclamation Theology,* p. 47.

[11]William A. Jones, Jr., "Back-door Divinity," *God in the Ghetto* (Elgin, Ill.: Progressive Baptist Publishing House, 1979), p. 124.

[12]Jones, "The Beasts and the Angels," *God in the Ghetto,* p. 137.

[13]Sandy F. Ray, "To Keep Footing in a Crumbling Culture," *Journeying Through a Jungle* (Nashville: Broadman Press, 1979), p. 50.

[14]*Ibid.,* p. 80.

[15]Manuel L. Scott, "Recipe for Racial Greatness," *The Gospel for the Ghetto* (Nashville: Broadman Press, 1973), p. 95.

[16]Scott, "The Ultimate in Urban Renewal," *The Gospel for the Ghetto,* pp. 28-29.

Selected Bibliography

Blassingame, John W., *The Slave Community: Plantation Life in the Antebellum South.* 2nd rev. enl. ed. New York: Oxford University Press, Inc., 1972.

Cone, James H., *A Black Theology of Liberation.* New York: Harper & Row, Publishers Inc., 1970.

————, *The Spirituals and the Blues: An Interpretation.* New York: The Seabury Press, Inc., 1972.

————, *God of the Oppressed.* New York: The Seabury Press, Inc., 1978.

Frazier, E. Franklin and Lincoln, C. Eric, *The Negro Church in America.* New York: Schocken Books, Inc., 1974.

King, Martin Luther, Jr., *Strength to Love.* Philadelphia: Fortress Press, 1981.

————, *Why We Can't Wait.* New York: Harper & Row, Publishers Inc., 1964.

————, *Where Do We Go from Here: Chaos or Community?* Harper & Row, Publishers Inc., 1967.

Lincoln, C. Eric and Frazier, E. Franklin, *The Black Church Since Frazier* (bound with *The Negro Church in America*). New York: Schocken Books, Inc., 1974.

Massey, Floyd, Jr., and McKinney, Samuel Berry, *Church Administration in the Black Perspective.* Valley Forge: Judson Press, 1976.

Mbiti, John S., *African Religions and Philosophy.* Garden City, New York: Anchor Books, 1970.

Mitchell, Ella Pearson, ed., *Those Preachin' Women.* Valley Forge: Judson Press, 1985.

Mitchell, Henry H., *Black Preaching.* New York: Harper & Row, Publishers Inc., 1979.

_____ , *The Recovery of Preaching.* San Francisco: Harper & Row, Publishers Inc., 1977.

Philpot, William M., *Best Black Sermons.* Valley Forge: Judson Press, 1972.

Proctor, Samuel D., and Watley, William D., *Sermons from the Black Pulpit.* Valley Forge: Judson Press, 1984.

Ray, Sandy F., *Journeying Through a Jungle.* Nashville: Broadman Press, 1979.

Roberts, J. Deotis, *Roots of a Black Future: Family and Church.* Philadelphia: The Westminister Press, 1980.

_____ , "The Hermeneutic Circle of Black Theology." An unpublished article written in summer 1980.

Sanders, James A., *God Has a Story Too.* Philadelphia: Fortress Press, 1979.

_____ , "Hermeneutics," *The Interpreter's Dictionary of the Bible,* supplementary volume. Nashville: Abingdon Press, 1976.

Stallings, James O., *Telling the Story: Evangelism in Black Churches.* Valley Forge: Judson Press, 1988.

Valentine, Kristen B., and Valentine, D. E., *Interlocking Pieces: Twenty Questions for Understanding Literature,* 2nd ed. Dubuque, Iowa: Kendall/Hunt Publishing Co., 1980.

Walker, Wyatt T., *"Somebody's Calling My Name."* Valley Forge: Judson Press, 1979.

Wilmore, Gayraud S., and Cone, James H., eds., *Black Theology: A Documentary History, 1966-1979.* Maryknoll, New York: Orbis Books, 1979.

Wimberly, Edward P., *Pastoral Counseling and Spiritual Values: A Black Point of View.* Nashville: Abingdon Press, 1982.

Wink, Walter, *The Bible in Human Transformation: Towards a New Paradigm for Biblical Study.* Philadelphia: Fortress Press, 1980.

DATE DUE

The Library Store   #47-0103